Starting Your
Television Writing Career

The Television Series

Robert J. Thompson, *Series Editor*

Other titles in the Television Series

Cue the Bunny on the Rainbow: Tales from TV's Most Prolific Sitcom Director
    Alan Rafkin

"Deny All Knowledge": Reading the X Files
    David Lavery, Angela Hague, and Marla Cartwright, eds.

Dictionary of Teleliteracy: Television's 500 Biggest Hits, Misses, and Events
    David Bianculli

Framework: A History of Screenwriting in the American Film. Third Edition.
    Tom Stempel

Laughs, Luck . . . and Lucy: How I Came to Create the Most Popular Sitcom of All Time
    Jess Oppenheimer, with Gregg Oppenheimer

Prime Time, Prime Movers: From I Love Lucy to L.A. Law—
    America's Greatest TV Shows and the People Who Created Them
    David Marc and Robert J. Thompson

Prime-Time Authorship: Works about and by Three TV Dramatists
    Douglas Heil

Rod Serling's Night Gallery: An After-Hours Tour
    Scott Skelton and Jim Benson

Storytellers to the Nation: A History of American Television Writing
    Tom Stempel

Teleliteracy: Taking Television Seriously
    David Bianculli

Television's Second Golden Age: From Hill Street Blues to ER
    Robert J. Thompson

TV Creators: Conversations with America's Top Producers
    of Television Drama. Volumes 1 and 2
    James L. Longworth, Jr.

Watching TV: Six Decades of American Television. Second Edition
    Harry Castleman and Walter Podrazik

The West Wing: The American Presidency as Television Drama
    Peter C. Rollins and John E. O'Connor, eds.

Abby Finer and Deborah Pearlman

Starting Your Television Writing Career

The Warner Bros. Television Writers Workshop Guide

"Feel the Burn" outline and script from *The George Lopez Show* written by Luisa Leschin. Created by Bruce Helford and George Lopez and Robert Borden.

"Birthday Boy" outline and script from *Without a Trace* written by Hank Steinberg. Created by Hank Steinberg.

Syracuse University Press

Published by Syracuse University Press
Syracuse, New York 13244–5160

The paper used in this publication meets the minimum requirements of American
National Standard for Information Sciences—Permanence of Paper for Printed Library
Materials, ANSI Z39.48–1984.∞™

Library of Congress Cataloging-in-Publication Data

Finer, Abby.
Starting your television writing career : the Warner Bros. television writers workshop guide /
Abby Finer and Deborah Pearlman.— 1st ed.
p. cm.— (The television series)
Includes bibliographical references and index.
ISBN 0–8156–0831–4 (alk. paper)
1. Television authorship. 2. Television authorship—Vocational guidance. I. Pearlman,
Deborah, 1965– II. Warner Bros. III. Title. IV. Series.
PN1992.7.F55 2004
808.2'25—dc22
2004017002

Manufactured in the United States of America

This book is intended for nonprofessional writers
trying to break into the television business.

Abby Finer has worked in television for more than twelve years in scripted and nonscripted programming. She is an executive producer of the comedy cable series, *Kenny vs. Spenny*, which airs in the United States and Canada. Abby resigned from the Warner Bros. Television Writers Workshop in 2003, and she currently resides in New York City.

Deborah Pearlman has been working with television writers since 1989. She has worked for USA Network and Bright Kauffman Crane *(Friends)* and has been director of the Warner Bros. Television Writers Workshop since 2001.

Contents

Sample Outlines and Scripts

Voices of Experience

Acknowledgments

Like any business, the television industry can be tough. Yet it's a lot of fun and immensely rewarding. We have been fortunate to have learned from and been in the company of so many incredibly talented people that it's hard to thank everybody, but here goes:

At Warner Bros. Television, many thanks to: Peter Roth for his undying support of the Workshop. Craig Hunegs for recognizing our idea and setting the wheels in motion. Jody Zucker for his enthusiasm, encouragement, and excellent advice. Sam Wolfson and Steve Fogelson without whose guidance we might have ended up in arbitration—or worse. Len Goldstein without whom there would not be a Drama Workshop. David Sacks, whose unique perspective and dedication has made this Workshop the most sought-after program for aspiring writers.

The Drama Team: Susan Rovner, Rachel Kaplan, Andrew Plotkin, Lisa Roos, Amy Reisenbach, and Richie Schwartz.

The Comedy Team: Marianne Cracchiolo, Lisa Lang, Wendy Steinhoff, Amy Byer, Rebecca Palatnick, and Susan Witterschein.

The Current Team (past and present): Melinda Hage, Clancy Collins, Adrienne Turner, Odetta Watkins, Rachel Filippelli, Stephanie Groves, Jeanne Cotton, Rebecca Franko, and Kim Metcalf.

To all of the assistants who help make everything so much easier.

Special thanks to Paula Allen, Gus Blackmon, Barbara Brogolitti,

Jeri Gray, Barry Meyer, Geriann McIntosh, Bruce Rosenblum, and Lee Spragens.

Very special thanks to Skye Van Raalte-Herzog, who helped us navigate the publishing world and became a friend in the process.

Many thanks to the Workshop volunteers: Fred Rubin, who has helped so many struggling writers find their voices and their stories. David Kelsey, the best intern in the world.

To all of the writers who have taken time from their busy schedules to speak to our classes, read scripts, give notes, meet our writers, and even hire many of them.

To all of the agents, managers, and their assistants for all that they do.

At Syracuse University Press, series editor Robert Thompson who took this project on before we even wrote one word and Peter Webber, director, and his entire staff at Syracuse University Press for guiding us through the process.

Very heartfelt thanks to Loan Dang, our publishing lawyer, who was always available to us and explained everything every step of the way.

Family thanks from Abby to: Allan and Denise, whose support, spirit, and enthusiasm inspire me every day. Marlene, who's always there for me. Fern, for having so much faith in me, and Justin and Greg Karch, who keep me laughing. Steven and Alex, for their unconditional love and support, which never ceases to amaze me; you are my family, too.

Family thanks from Deborah to: Steve for always pushing me to follow my dreams. Brian and Evan for understanding that sometimes Mom has to work. Nonie, who fills in all the holes in my life. And very special thanks to E. Jack Kaplan, who is a terrific writer and an even better dad.

Introduction

The Warner Bros. Television Writers Workshop initially started in 1976, as the brainchild of Gus Blackmon, an executive in the Story Department of what is now Warner Bros. Television. He thought it would behoove the company to train writers and try to get them hired on our TV shows—in essence, to create a farm system. With this training, ultimately these writers would produce their own shows for years to come, which would benefit both the writer and the studio. Blackmon put the word out to literary agencies, and scripts immediately started arriving. Initially, the program was geared toward minorities, but today the Workshop includes men and women of all walks of life. In 1984, when the sitcom genre was king of the airwaves, the Workshop focused solely on the writing of the half-hour comedy. The success of the Comedy Workshop prompted the installment of the Drama Workshop, which became a separate entity in 1998.

Over the years, both the Comedy and Drama Workshops have evolved into the premiere program for aspiring television writers to get training in a professional environment and have a foray into the job market. They're highly regarded throughout the television creative community as a tremendous source of talent for those in a position to represent or hire writers for television shows.

The success rate of the Workshops continues to be astounding.

Graduates from our program are currently working on shows such as *Without a Trace, Scrubs, The Sopranos,* and *Joey,* just to name a few. With the ongoing, incredible support from Warner Bros. Television and all of its producers, the writers who experience the Workshop get a first-class education and a unique opportunity to pursue their craft and career.

Each year, the Warner Bros. Television Writers Workshop receives scripts from people all over the United States, Canada, and even a few countries overseas. All of these aspiring writers hope that their script will be considered good enough to move on to the next step—an interview that could lead to acceptance in either the Comedy or the Drama Workshop. In the past few seasons, we have received nearly one thousand submissions for both Workshops.

For our most recent Workshops, we narrowed down the field by meeting with about thirty people for each category. All of these writers had demonstrated solid writing ability in their submissions. From there, we chose thirteen people to actually participate in either the Comedy or the Drama Workshop. The competition is always tough. Not only did these writers have to have great scripts, but they also needed to have the type of personality that we feel producers would respond to and hire. Quiet, shy types had a difficult time making an impression. Overeager, know-it-all types were rejected. Sometimes, admittedly, we are proved wrong. But our instincts and experience help us recognize writers who can't or won't deliver.

It's our job at the Workshop to find up-and-coming writing talent for the studio's comedy and drama television shows. We assist the Warner Bros. Television creative departments, as well as the studio's producers and production companies who create shows. The Workshop participants gain exposure that is envied by those trying to break into the business of writing for television. Because of the intense training writers receive, the top literary agents, television executives, and producers seek out those who have been selected to participate in the Workshop for the possibility of hiring them for a staff writing position. These writers are commonly known as baby or staff writers.

Why we wrote this book

As frequent lecturers, we were constantly being asked if we could recommend a book to help new writers. We found that there were no comprehensive resources available that really spelled out the guidelines needed to pursue a career in television writing. We hope this book will fill that void.

Television Writing Today

1.

So You Want to Be a TV Writer . . .

According to a recent study, there are approximately fifty-six hundred writers working in television today. Each one of those writers could tell you a different story about how they got into the business of writing for television. Some had a connection, whereas others lucked into it. Yet each and every one of them had to show a sample of their work to get that job. Nobody gets hired and stays hired just because they tell funny jokes or they are a powerful executive's nephew. They get jobs because they can demonstrate their talent by writing a good, solid script.

In order to be considered for a job on a show, your sample material must stand out among the thousands of scripts that are read each year by television agents, executives, and producers. This book is designed to give you the inside information on what is expected in TV scripts.

What is considered sample material?

A sample script is a way to show that you can take existing characters and design a story that makes sense in the format of a television script. Sounds easy enough, right?

The trick with writing sample material is to come up with a story based on the characters created by other writers. A valid sample is one that is written for a show that is currently on the air. So the tough part becomes picking the *right* show, choosing an *appropriate* story, and making the whole thing come together so that when someone reads it, they are imagining that this story is viable for that particular show.

Why is sample material important?

A terrific sample script is worth its weight in gold. A good script shows the creative community in the television business that you have talent, fortitude, and smarts, which are all very important skills in television writing. Everyone from agents to network executives is always on the lookout for that fresh new writing voice. And since most scripts are poorly written, the good ones really stand out and those writers are sought after.

What does it take to become a TV writer?

Writing for television is a fun and rewarding way to make a living. However, it requires a lot of hard work and dedication to make it in this business. You must have a thick skin and an open mind. You must be able to take criticism well, and most important, you must work well with others. Since most television writing is done as a group, a person who likes to work alone will not thrive in a staff situation.

The people who make it in television writing all have one thing in common: they love the medium of television. It's that passion for the small screen that carries them through the lean times. A new staff writer who is easy to work with and passionate about television will have a much better chance of succeeding than someone who thinks television is beneath their talent. That's not to say you won't ever write a feature or even have one optioned or produced. Our advice is just to concentrate on one or the other before tackling both. Become prolific in one medium, and the other will come calling.

We advise writers trying to decide between features and television to strongly consider television first. For one thing, television is a writer's medium. The most powerful person on any television show is the executive producer, who is usually also the head writer. Executive producers make decisions on everything from the sets to how the actors' hair should be styled. They are responsible for every detail of what you see and hear on-screen. In films, the director is the head honcho. The opposite is true of an executive producer. If they don't like the way a director is shooting something, they can hire a different director. Also, in the time it takes for a screenwriter to get his first film made (which can be *years*), a television writer could be a high-ranking producer on a television show making hundreds of thousands of dollars a year within a much shorter time span.

Now is a good time to mention that as a television writer working your way up the ladder, you will continue to write sample material. Let's say you get lucky and land a job writing for a so-so television show. It gets low ratings, but the network keeps it on because they don't have anything else to replace it. You work on that show for a season or two (after all, you have to pay the bills), and your agent tells you there is an opening on a more desirable show, a top-ten show. You should have a new piece of material ready to send out so you can show the people at the better show that you can write at their level. You certainly couldn't send your episode of the so-so show, because it won't measure up to the better show's standards.

Our Workshop participants have always been encouraged to write new samples even if they are working on shows. Knowing you can whip out strong material in a reasonable amount of time is a good way to prepare yourself for the unstable world of show business. And you know the old cliché: practice makes perfect.

Do I have to live in Los Angeles?

Yes. Trying to jump-start a career from anywhere but LA is nearly impossible, even if you have the best *Will & Grace* anyone has ever read.

However, you can practice your skills anywhere. At the Workshop a few seasons ago, we received a script sent from an army communications officer stationed in Afghanistan! Ultimately, you will have to move to southern California or you won't be taken seriously as a potential employee. Although the majority of shows are filmed in southern California, there are a few produced on the East Coast and in Canada, but nearly all of the writing staffs remain based in Los Angeles.

Once I write my sample script, can I send it to that show?

Absolutely not. Producers will not read sample material of a show they work on for several reasons. First, creatively, they know the show so well that they are known to be the harshest judges of that material. Second, there are legal reasons. If you sent a script with a story idea that the show's writers have been thinking about, the show can't use it for fear that you could sue them. Many shows receive scripts from the general public, and the show's employees are not permitted to even open the envelopes that appear to have scripts in them. Don't waste your time or theirs. Your script will not get read.

Also, do not send material to a network or a television production company or studio. Legally, these companies are prohibited from reading scripts that are not sent through the proper channels, that is, literary agents.

I have a great idea for a new series . . .

No. The purpose of a sample script is to show a perspective employer that you can take already existing characters and write a viable episode. That is what your job will be on a show. Your script is your audition. Nailing the style, format, dialogue, and storytelling of an existing show is the only way you can prove to anybody that you have the talent it takes to earn a spot on a writing staff. Then, after many years spent learning this format and writing other people's shows, you will, we hope, be paid handsomely for your original ideas.

If you have an original idea for which you'd like to write a script, by all means write it, but keep in mind that it should be used as a second or third backup sample of your work. Don't expect to launch your career with an original script.

Should I write comedy or drama?

The general rule is that half-hour shows are comedies, whereas one-hour shows are always considered dramas.

Obviously, you should try to choose the genre that you are most comfortable writing. If you love sitcoms, try to write one. If you like to tell stories in a longer format, you may find that you prefer drama. The best way to find out is to write one of each, because at the end of the day, it's a personal choice. Knowing what is required in each genre will also help make the decision become clearer. It will be easier if you try to sell yourself in one area rather than tackling both. Have your material evaluated by someone in the industry, if you can, to determine where your strength truly lies, and take into consideration which genre you are most passionate about. Many first-time writers think they are good at both comedy and drama. We have found that most beginning writers tend to be stronger in one genre than the other.

A word about comedy writers

People who write comedies are generally gregarious and natural storytellers. Also, they're people who can work well with others. Since comedy writing is a collaborative process, being a good listener is also very important. Generally, comedy writing staffs sit in a conference room for fourteen to eighteen hours a day, telling funny stories to each other. It's through this process that many ideas are born and eventually become your favorite episodes of television. For example, the writers on *Friends* spent a tremendous amount of time talking about things that happened in their lives to come up with realistic stories for the characters. Many of the things that happened to Rachel, Monica, Phoebe, Joey, Chandler, and Ross actually happened to the writers or someone the writers knew.

Comedy writers who have spoken to our Workshop liken their TV writing experience to live theater. There are many similarities. Like theater, sitcoms are performed in front of a live audience. Sitcom actors love it, because they get immediate reactions to what they are doing. Writers like it too, because if a joke isn't getting a laugh, they have a few minutes to come up with something better. It's important to realize that sitcom scripts are being rewritten right up to when the audience is being loaded in and the cameras are being put in place the night the show is being taped.

There also is a real sense of a "let's put on a show" kind of feeling. It takes about eighty people to put one episode of a half-hour television show on the air. So there are a lot of people working together for a common goal, and that's to make each episode the best one yet. That group effort gives each individual working on a show a strong sense of pride and belonging.

Writing staffs have changed a lot over the years. In the old days when television was a relatively new medium, writings staffs consisted of two or three, maybe four, writers. In the mid-1980s when comedies dominated the airwaves, the staffs were huge. Some shows had upward of twenty people writing the show. In recent years, the staffs have gotten smaller. The average number is currently between twelve and fourteen. Money isn't so abundant anymore, and drama shows are more dominant on network schedules. Comedy budgets have been slashed, and seasoned professionals who have been waiting for comedy to make a comeback have taken the few jobs out there, leaving little or no space for those trying to break into the sitcom business. But the climate of television changes year to year. And as networks pick up more sitcoms, the job market could open up again overnight.

A word about drama writers

Whereas comedy writers liken their experience to live theater, drama writers compare their experience to filmmaking. For starters, scripts are usually completed before shooting begins, so there is no scrambling to make something work, like the comedy writers do on their shows. Unless their individual episode is being filmed, the entire writing staff is not present on location or on a set. Drama writers also tend to work in a more secluded environment. There is still a "writers' room" where the entire staff comes together to brainstorm story ideas, but the actual writing is usually done by a solitary writer, who then receives direction from the executive producer.

2.

Choosing the Right Show and Doing Research

How to pick the right series for your script

This is the first crucial decision that you make when writing sample material. There are a variety of things to consider when choosing the show that is right for you. Here are some tips:

Pick a show you like

There is nothing worse than trying to write a sample for a show that you don't even like. We have seen people in the Workshop try to write a show they have no interest in, and it really shows. Writing is hard enough, so pick a show that you genuinely are a fan of and perhaps watch often. This is an area where people really overthink the process. They think if they write something obscure, they will stand out, because every other writer is writing the same top-five shows. Nonsense. What makes a script stand out is a clever story that is well executed. Period.

Tastes great vs. less filling

The equivalent to that adage in the scriptwriting world is popular vs. critically acclaimed. Some writers choose what show to write by checking out the weekly top-twenty shows and picking one of those. Others read reviews and see which shows aren't necessarily popular but are critically acclaimed. You will be on the right track as long as you can confirm two things: the general public is very familiar with the show, and it's a show that's going to have some longevity.

Wait and see

It's always good to choose a show that has been on the air for at least one full year. A sample is only good as long as the show is on the air, so choose wisely. On the flip side, don't choose a show that is clearly on its way out, either. You'll work hard on a script that will be worthless in a few months.

Research

Once you have chosen your show, you can breathe a huge sigh of relief and relax . . . but then you have to roll up your sleeves. The next phase is to research your show, and there are several good ways to do it.

Watch TV

You will need to record at least eight to ten shows. If you pick a popular show that is still airing original episodes and also happens to be in syndication, you will be able to collect them rather quickly.

If you are going to write a critically acclaimed current show that may not be airing in syndication, that's fine, but just plan to collect those episodes over a longer period of time. Even if you think you know your show inside and out, watch all of those episodes again. You need to study these shows in a way that you don't when you watch them for pure enjoyment. In fact, we recommend that you watch the shows in close succession and take written notes of the following:

- What kinds of stories are they telling?
- Which characters are the stories mostly about?

- How many scenes are in each episode?
- How soon does the story start? When does each story reach its climactic moment? Where is the act break? How do the stories end?
- See if there are speech patterns for each character.
- Are there frequently used expressions? Make sure your script includes them to make it authentic.
- Look at what the actors can do. For example, if in a comedy series, are they experts in physical comedy? Can you write an episode that showcases that particular talent?
- Be aware of the sets the show uses. This is particularly important in sitcoms that are completely filmed on soundstages. Try to write shows that include existing sets, not new ones specifically for your script.

This research will provide a road map as you are creating your story. It will also come in very handy when you are writing your script. By envisioning the characters in your head, your script will have a familiarity that will be very appealing to the reader, whomever it may be. It will feel and sound like the show you have chosen, and that's the main goal.

Web sites

Research can also be conducted on the Internet. All of the network Web sites have information on their respective shows, and many of them have a list of the stories they have already completed, which is commonly referred to as an episodic guide. You should try not to write the same story line if it has already been done.

We have found that some of the most detailed sites are the ones updated by the fans. Some sites may even include some back story on the characters. Others have transcripts. After investigating the network's Web site, try typing in the show's name in various search engines for more listings.

Get a real script from a show

We encourage you to try to obtain at least one produced script from the show you have chosen, so that you can see how it looks and reads on paper. Some scripts from popular shows are sold as content in published books. A produced script will give you an idea of the format and structure of the show, as well as approximately how many pages the show you want to write for normally consists of. It's okay to write just a few pages more or a few pages less.

Go to a taping

If you happen to live in or visit the Los Angeles area, try to go a show taping. Audiences Unlimited (http://www.tvtickets.com or http://www.tvtixs.com [818–653–4105]) is a service that offers free tickets to tapings of sitcoms that have audiences. It's a good way to see what actually happens on a soundstage set. Tickets can also be purchased in advance through the Museum of Television and Radio's Web site at http://www.mtr.org.

3.

It All Starts with Story

Coming up with a story line for either a comedy or a drama is the most crucial step in writing a great script. A well-structured story is one that has a clear beginning, middle, and end.

First and foremost, the stories should deal with the needs and desires of the main characters. It's best to set up the story's conflict within the first few pages of the script to grab the interest of the reader. The main character should want something (the beginning), obstacles get in the way of achieving that goal (the middle), and finally, the character accomplishes the goal and most likely gains some kind of new insight (the end). In addition, the story should also contain unexpected twists and rising complications, while each scene moves the story forward.

What should the episode be about?

The episode should be a typical "day in the life" of the show. In other words, you should write everyday stories. One must keep in mind that a produced episode provides us with a visual experience. Your script is to be *read*, and it is important that it be consistent with the show and its characters, as well as move along easily.

Every year we receive scripts that will likely be eliminated because of the common story mistakes we have listed below:

Don't write an episode revolving around holidays or special occasions. This is an area reserved for those who are actually writing on the show. In television, they are known as "easy outs" because holidays usually make for emotionally charged episodes. Obviously, the three big holidays (Thanksgiving, Christmas, and Easter) but also some of the smaller holidays like Valentine's Day, Halloween, and even birthdays are poor story choices.

Don't write episodes that involve life-changing events for the characters. That includes pregnancies, births, deaths, weddings, or divorces.

Don't create stories about the arrival of the long-lost relative or ex-lover. It feels trite.

Don't have stories involving natural disasters, including blackouts, storms, or earthquakes.

Don't do the "very special episode" in which the characters have to deal with addictions, amnesia, or dream sequences.

How to come up with story ideas

The creative process is very personal, and each artist has his or her own process. Some people are comfortable working alone. Some people prefer bouncing ideas off other creative people. In other words, there is no one right way to be creative.

Here are a few helpful ways to jump-start your creative process:

Read. Keep up with what's going on in the world, be it through a major metropolitan newspaper or a small community bulletin. Both are filled with stories that may spark a story idea. Magazines are also a good way to stimulate your brain. Just flipping through a range of different magazines can lead you to an interesting story idea or visual image. For this kind of brainstorming, you must let your mind free-associate as you skim through the images.

Look in the mirror. You are your own treasure trove of stories. Think back on situations in your life that can be translated into a script.

Open your eyes and ears. Be aware of your surroundings. Notice how people talk and how they act in certain situations. Keep a notebook handy to jot down observations so you can refer to them later.

Brainstorming. Talking with friends and family about their experiences can provide a new perspective on a familiar theme. Most shows you see on television stem from an event that happened to either that writer or someone that writer knows. It's your job to take that story and try to fit it into the style of the show you have chosen.

Try not to analyze each idea that pops into your head, because that could stop the creative flow. It's best not to linger too long on one particular idea, but, rather, keep your mind moving along, as you can always go back to some of the earlier ideas at a later time to see if they generate a story. Just know that some ideas are just not going to work, and that's okay. Concentrate on about seven to ten ideas per story line. Next, try to come up with just a few sentences to describe all of your ideas while establishing a clear beginning, middle, and end.

Following these techniques will help prepare you for the next stage in this process: further developing your story into an outline.

Did I choose the right story?

Study your ideas, be critical, and, above all, trust your instincts. After determining which ideas would make good stories, ask yourself the following questions to make sure you are off to a good start:

- Is this story different from what has been seen before?
- Is the idea logical, and is it suited for the show you've chosen?
- Does the story truly have a beginning, middle, and end?
- Is the conflict really strong? Does the conflict get more complicated?
- Are the main characters being used in the main story?

You can test your idea to see if it is working by creating a logline. A logline is usually one or two sentences that sum up the entire episode. If you can clearly establish a beginning, middle, and end in the logline, your story will probably work. The middle is where most people have a problem. Make sure the story's conflict has reached a critical point, and you will have a good middle part for your story.

Once you have chosen your story, you are ready to write your outline. Up until this stage, all of the above information is applicable to both comedy and drama scripts. The outline stage is where this road splits. If you are writing a sitcom, continue to "The Situation Comedy," or if you are writing a drama, please skip to "The One-Hour Drama."

The Situation Comedy

4.

Starting the Writing Process

Before you get excited that you have a story that will make a killer sample, it has to survive some very difficult stages. This process is designed to expose the problems of your story at each developmental stage. Although your story may make sense in theory, it might not work so well as you further develop it. Don't be alarmed if at any given time in this process you have to take a step backward and rework a story element or even your entire idea. If your story is not right at the outline stage, writing the script will be ten times harder. So get it right early. The one thing every comedy writer knows:

If You Don't Have Conflict, You Don't Have a Story.

Although there are variations on how conflict is portrayed, it is always present. How much conflict and how the characters deal with it are completely up to you as the writer. However, you must remember to stay in the format of the series you have chosen.

Structure

Pick any comedy and watch one episode. You will see that in the first scene, the main character establishes a goal. He or she will spend the next twenty-two minutes trying to get what he or she wants, creating more obstacles in the process. To better illustrate this, review the simple format known as the tree analogy, a commonly used device:

ACT I

1. The character establishes a goal. (The character wants to climb to the top of a tree.)
2. The character is confronted with the first obstacle. (Halfway up the tree the character discovers a beehive.)
3. Things get worse (there are more obstacles) for the character. (Trying to get away from the bees, the character realizes he is stuck in the tree.)

ACT BREAK

ACT II

1. Complications arise; things get worse before they get better. (The bees start to sting him, and he is allergic to bee stings, so he climbs out on a thin branch.)
2. Twists and turns occur as a result of the complications. (It starts to rain, and the bees go away. Now the character is stuck in a tree in a storm.)
3. Resolution. (The character figures out a way to get out of the tree.)

It's important to note that the character is active in his role of figuring out the problem. Many novice writers rely on some outside random circumstance that gets the character out of the situation. The best stories are when the main character is proactive in the resolution.

Most sitcoms have two different story lines happening in each script. The A-story involves the main characters, and the B-story centers around the secondary characters. Both stories should be put through the tree analogy to make sure they include the all-important beginning, middle, and end.

If you can jot down story points (also known as "beats") using the tree analogy as your guide, you will have completed what is known as a beat sheet. Once you have these key points of your story written out, you will begin to see your script take shape. When your beat sheet is completed, you can move on the next phase, which is writing an outline.

Outlines

Before you write the script, it's important to know that the story really works on every level. You will write in a form you are already comfortable with, which is prose. To write a story you are not sure works in an entirely new form (dialogue) is very difficult. A detailed outline is the best way to determine if the story works. In fact, all story flaws should be caught and addressed in the outline. Once you get your outline correctly done, writing the script is easy, so we encourage you to not bypass this important step. If your structure is wrong and you write the script anyway, you are building on quicksand.

If you consider skipping this step and diving right into writing your script (as we know many of you do), consider this quick reference list of the importance of an outline:

- It identifies structural problems in the story.
- It helps you see if the story works and make sure the story is advancing in every scene. (If you remove a scene and the story still works, then you know that scene isn't necessary.)
- It determines if your characters appear in each scene that they are supposed to be in, as well as helping to check entrances and exits of those characters.
- It helps you ensure that the characters enter a scene with one attitude and leave with a slightly different one by the end of the scene.
- It determines if your act breaks work.
- It checks the flow and pacing of the story lines.

We have included a sample from *The George Lopez Show* in chapter 8 of this book for you to study and review. Although each show may have its own way of doing outlines, this is a good example to use as a guide.

All in all, an outline is basically a road map, tracking the story scene by scene. It explains the "drive" of each scene and shows the characters' attitudes throughout the show. Also, you will notice that there is some dialogue in the provided outline. Not too much, but just enough to illustrate a funny joke or comment.

The first draft

The first draft is the first time you see your story in script form. We suggest you write the first draft as quickly as possible without getting hung up on jokes, stage directions, or other details of the script. As you write, if you find that your story is not working, there is most likely something wrong with the story that was not apparent, or even ignored, in the outline stage. If this is the case, you must go back and make adjustments so the story makes sense.

You should make sure your story tracks from one scene to the next. To say a story tracks is to say that it follows a logical order. For example, if scene A ends with your lead character walking out the door in a huff to confront someone, scene B shouldn't start with that same character happily baking a cake. It's not logical. It will feel wrong because it doesn't make sense.

The next trouble area is starting the story early enough. Since we have established that there is no story without conflict, the story doesn't start until the conflict has been identified. The conflict has to be introduced by page 3.

Because the whole idea of this format is to draw in the audience and make them curious enough to see how and where the story ends, make sure the act break is in the right place. The act break also needs to be strong enough to keep the readers interested in what happens next—the "uh-oh" moment. Many scripts lose readers at this point because the story hasn't progressed to a logical climax or the climax is not satisfying enough.

Scenes

Make sure the scenes in your first draft are driven by the lead character(s). Scenes, like the story itself, should have a beginning, middle, and end. Remember, each scene must advance the story, so new and relevant facts need to emerge, giving the characters something to talk and joke about. A good way to test the sequence of the story by scene is to remove a scene that might not be fitting in with the rest of the story. Again, if you remove a scene and the story still makes sense, then you didn't need that scene in the first place.

It's also important to remember that the characters drive the scenes. Make sure each character goes through some kind of change during each scene. It doesn't have to be a big mood swing, but a shift of some kind is a good indication that the story is progressing.

Remember, try to construct scenes that:

1. push the story forward,
2. expose an attitude, and
3. are hysterically funny.

As mentioned earlier, the act break is what we refer to as the "uh-oh moment." When we return from the act break (which is essentially a commercial break), we continue to build the tension in the first scene of the second act. The action should hit its stride about halfway through the second act, so that the conflict in the story comes to a head. A clear resolution should occur during the last half of the second act, just as the problem is at its highest crisis point. The ending should come about as the result of the main character(s)' actions and should not be coincidental or obvious. If the script is written in three acts, then the first act should establish and begin to build the conflict, whereas the second act contains the main act break and the third the resolution.

Also noteworthy is the block comedy scene, a term that describes the big physical comedic scene of a show. The block comedy scene usually comes in act II, before the resolution. During the research phase of this process, you should make note if the series you chose uses this device. If it does, you should use it in your script as well.

Characters

Keep the story simple, but allow the characters to be multidimensional and complex. Show that you understand and can capture the voices of the show's main characters accurately. The character(s) should not just react to the problem but, rather, drive the story.

Writing with emotion that demonstrates a character's feelings beneath a situation is a surefire way to get attention with your script. Clarify all the characters' attitudes in every scene, and make sure their motivations are true to what's already been established in the series.

It's also important to make the A-story focus on the main characters. Scripts that don't follow this rule never seem to recover, no matter how funny they are. Remember, the idea here is to mimic what you see on television. Don't get fancy and try to come up with a new character to serve as a challenge to the main character. This device never really works in a sample situation and should not be attempted.

Another area writers tend to ignore is the entrances and exits of the characters. You need to give the characters a reason for coming and going within a scene. The reasons could be as simple as passing through one room to another or coming to get an item left in the room. You should also track your characters as they enter a scene thinking or feeling one way and shifting (if ever so slightly) their attitudes in a different direction by the end of that scene. When a major character leaves a scene, allow him or her to leave the scene with a funny joke.

Characters are also more interesting if they are not only talking, but also doing something while they talk. The action may offer some additional humor. Even the most mundane actions can offer some humor or irony, if it's somehow related to the dialogue.

Dialogue

The dialogue should reflect how the characters' voices are on the show and how the characters talk to each other; they shouldn't just trade funny lines back and forth. Remember to make the characters sound real. Many novice writers try to be funny with every line, which isn't really how people talk to one another.

Dialogue should be used to advance each scene as well as the overall plot, while revealing something about the character. It should also convey conflict and connect scenes. And, of course, the dialogue has to be funny. Laughs stem from the dialogue that comes from the characters as they tackle their situation.

Also, try to stay away from clichés and phrases we have heard a million times before. Phrases like "Houston, we have a problem" are lame and should not appear in your script.

Humor

Determining whether something is funny is subjective. But clever, funny jokes that evoke a smile, a chuckle, or a laugh from a reader's perspective will put your script in the "I need to meet this writer" category. Humor also pertains to the story. You need to ask yourself what is funny about the story. If the idea is funny in a simple logline, then go for it.

The best jokes come from the characters and story, and they should be organic to what is happening. Humor often comes from a negative place, as jokes can highlight the conflict. Jokes should also help move the story along. Therefore, don't get too attached to your jokes, as they can stop a scene too. Don't fill scenes with jokes or physical comedy that has nothing to do with any of the story lines. Remember, the story must advance with every line in a script, so don't stop the flow of a scene for a joke. Be ruthless by keeping only the jokes that move the story, expose a character's attitude, are funny, and have emotion. Jokes that are lacking on one or more of these elements should not stay in your script.

Although it seems very hard to get rid of jokes you like, just know that it can really work against you to keep them, particularly if you are trying to work a story around the jokes. That can get you into a lot of trouble. It's far better to focus on and master the craft of writing good stories and providing solid structure, rather than writing some funny jokes. As industry readers, we consider story first and foremost.

Try to make your setup and punch line tight, and place the latter at the end of a speech. As we've mentioned, each scene should end with a very funny line, which should be said by one of the stars of the show. This is known as a scene blow, and it should be a hard-hitting joke, usually about the character's change of attitude, and relevant to the story. An act blow comes at the end of the first act, whereas the last line of dialogue is often called a show or curtain blow.

The best shows not only have funny dialogue, but also utilize the skills of their actors who can perform physical comedy as well. This, of course, depends on the show and its cast. Keep in mind that being funny requires that you have the talent for it, because even understanding what makes something funny isn't the same as being able to *be* funny.

Exposition

Exposition refers to the information that the reader must know in order to follow what is happening in the story. Expositional dialogue reveals information about the plot and the characters. If you find that a story suffers if expositional dialogue is removed, just make sure there isn't another place to put it. If plot and character information can be shown through images rather than dialogue, it would be beneficial, as it is better to *show* than to *tell*. Exposition should be worked into a story in small doses so that the story keeps moving.

Find a way to bring out exposition in an interesting way that doesn't get lost in long-winded speeches. If your characters are yelling at each other, disguise it with humor and jokes. Exposition can be inserted into dialogue through conflict, particularly when angry words are spoken.

Visual

Often, writers are so busy focusing on all of the other important elements that they tend to overlook what the audience might be watching while the dialogue is being spoken. Making a scene visually interesting will make your script look very polished. Place the characters in interesting situations while they engage in conversation.

Story and structure questions

We hope that at this point you have completed your first draft. We have created a list of hard-hitting questions you need to ask yourself to make sure your story works, the voices are accurate, and everything else seems to be in order.

- Does your script contain the right amount of stories for the show you are writing?
- Are the stories focused and well developed?
- Have you told a fresh story with a solid payoff, or is the story boring?
- Is each story logical?
- Does the main story begin early?
- Is the dramatic conflict strong in each story line?
- Do any scenes lag, or are any scenes redundant?
- Are the scenes built upon each other in a logical sequence of dramatic action?
- Do you have too many story lines? (This problem pertains primarily to drama but can occur in comedy too.)
- Does each scene reveal some kind of emotion?
- Are scenes overwrought with exposition?
- Are the scenes the right length?

- Are there enough twists and turns?
- Does anything happen that feels too convenient or obvious?
- Is the resolution too obvious, or is there a satisfying ending?

Character questions

- Are every action and reaction justified? Is each character's motivation clear?
- Do the characters' attitudes track from scene to scene smoothly?
- Is there a reason for each character to be included in a scene, and does he or she have something to say?
- Are the characters' voices accurate?
- Are they talking to each other and not just trading funny lines?
- Have the characters revealed a variety of emotions?

Dialogue questions

- Have you been tough in judging your jokes?
- Have you cut jokes that aren't funny?
- Is the dialogue too wordy or too long?
- Did each scene end with a funny line told by a main character?

Tips for a final check

After going through this checklist, and having identified the areas that need improvement, take another pass at the script and address these issues. Once you have done so, you now have a second draft. It's time to put the finishing touches on your script.

If possible, get a group of friends together and assign them to play the various characters in order to read your script out loud. This is what a show does with its cast and is known as a table read. Make a note of which jokes work and which don't get a chuckle. You can also just read it aloud yourself and tape it. Listening to the tape may present some problems that you would pick up on only if you heard the script aloud rather than just reading it over and over. Regardless of what method you use, take the opportunity to really hone your script and make it great.

Polish, formatting, and looking professional

To polish a script means to take a final look at the details. Go through each line of dialogue to make sure the story is advancing. This is an opportunity to punch up the jokes and make sure they are as strong as possible.

As far as formatting, make sure to use screenwriting software. There are plenty on the market that will make your experience much easier. We suggest Final Draft, which is one of the most popular and easy to use scriptwriting programs because it provides a ready-made format for nearly all current television shows.

You have worked so hard on your script, making sure everything works, so it would be a shame for someone to pick it up, read one page, and put it aside because of a typo. Unfortunately, that happens all the time. Your script should look as professional as possible. It should be printed on clean white three-hole-punched paper and then bound with two industry-standard brads (Acco brand no. 5 or no. 6), one in each of the first and third holes. If your local stationery store does not carry them, consider buying them on-line. Do not bind your script in any other way or it will look amateurish.

It is recommended that you obtain, either through contacts or by purchasing, a script of the show you have chosen to write. Each show has its own style, and you want to do your best in duplicating it. There should be a cover on the script that has the name of the show, the episode's title, the writer's name, and the writer's contact information. You do not need to include a cast list or any other production information.

You should also register your script on-line with the Writers Guild of America, which has two Web sites, http://www.wga.org for the West Coast and http://www.wgaeast.org for the rest of the country. Or you can register with the U.S. Copyright Office (call 202-207-9100 to find out how) prior to sending your script to an industry contact.

Our last words of advice are not to let the script leave your hands until you are absolutely sure it is the best that you can do. Become a perfectionist if you aren't one already.

The One-Hour Drama

5.

Choosing the Right Show

The great thing about dramatic television is there are so many different kinds of shows. Finding the right show for you to write should be relatively easy. Think about the various types of drama shows. Since you will eventually need two samples, we urge you to consider showing a variety of writing by choosing different types. The different drama genres are:

The Family Drama — These are usually softer shows that focus on a family ensemble. Current examples include *The Gilmore Girls, Everwood,* and *Six Feet Under.* These shows tend to deal with relationships and emotional issues and are told in large, sweeping story arcs, making them a more serialized style of storytelling.

The Procedural — These shows are driven entirely by the week-to-week incoming story. In other words, the stories in *Without a Trace* revolve around the missing person, not the people who are investigating the missing person.

The Office Ensemble — *The West Wing* and *ER* are at their cores office ensembles. They take a group of professionals and tell stories about not only their work, but also how their work affects their personal lives.

The Fantasy or Sci-Fi — These shows include anything dealing with the supernatural or superheroes or highlighting the fantasy element. For example, *Smallville* fits in this category.

Beat sheets

Once you have chosen the series, you must focus on the stories. The first step is to get your story ideas on paper and list the key points. This is called a beat sheet.

A beat sheet is an abbreviated version of scenes that don't contain dialogue. Although it is more commonly used in comedy writing, it is a good way of organizing your story points. On a sheet of paper, jot down a few bulleted points of what happens in each scene. This sheet will help you see if you have structurally sound stories. Take the time to do this step and then move on to the outline stage.

Another way to test if your story is working structurally is to put each scene on an index card. This serves as an alternative to a beat sheet. On each card, indicate where the scene takes place, the characters in the scene, and what story point needs to be made. Do not include any dialogue. You should be able to determine if every scene does something to drive the story forward and reveals important elements or character revelations.

Structure and scene writing

Structure is the blueprint of your script. Drama scripts are presented in a four-act structural format, often with a teaser and tag (a separate opening and closing).

The first scene should establish what the main story is about, while the pacing of each subsequent scene advances the story, making the conflict more and more intense and more developed. The first scene is the most difficult to write.

Like each story, each scene should have a clearly established beginning, middle, and end. Breaking this down further, each scene contains new developments, better known as a story beat. A story beat is an event; it indicates that something has happened. Many writers use this term when discussing scenes.

Because most shows utilize at least three plotlines, the A-story is what the episode is mainly about (if it's a medical drama, there might be a crisis that affects the entire hospital). The B-story usually features characters involved in a personal-type story line. Finally, a C-story is usually lighter in tone and is often used as comic relief. Again, it's best to become an expert on the particular show you are writing and study its stories, because it may follow a different format.

Within each story, there are complications—obstacles that the characters must endure. As the story develops, you need to ask yourself, "What would happen if. . . ?" Exploring every option is a great way to come up with some innovative twists. Try a variety of different possibilities.

John McNamara (of *Lois & Clark* and *The Fugitive*) is an executive producer who has lectured at the Workshop many times. He has a wonderful paradigm that has helped countless beginning writers (and some professionals too) to understand dramatic structure. It's based on the concept that in order to keep people interested in the script, the stories must build incrementally throughout. By breaking the main story down into four distinct sections you can easily make sure your story works. (Remember, each episode will have more than one story, so make sure you use this model for the B- and C-stories as well.)

Teaser—This is where the character's goal must be established. It is referred to as the "gotta" or the "I want" part of the story. You are setting up what the character wants so there can be conflict when he can't get what he wants. Simply put, it is the beginning of the story.

Act I—This is where the complications start to come in; it's what McNamara refers to as the "uh-oh" act. A dramatic event occurs that gets in the way of the character's goal.

Act II—The "Oh my God" act is where the character is in a situation where it's quite possible he won't get out of it, or at the very least, you wonder how he is going to get out of it. Act II is the most important part of the story because if you end it correctly, you have the reader invested in the story, and they will want to see how it ends.

Act III—Things start to let up a bit, and the resolution or possibility of a resolution is introduced here. Continuing the escalation in Act III is a risk because oftentimes you will not have enough time to end your story without feeling rushed.

Act IV—Whew! The crisis has been resolved, and it feels organic and true to the story.

Remember, the conflict should continue to rise after each act break. Most people let the action or suspense continue halfway through the middle of Act III so Act IV is not all resolution. A very common error among writers is to not make the act break strong enough. Often, the "Oh my God" moment happens too soon, making the rest of the episode feel slow and boring. Sometimes the "big moment" doesn't arrive until too late in the script. If that's the case, it should be moved up earlier in the draft so that it will function correctly as an act break.

Once you have *broken* your story, it's very important to write it in a format in which you are most comfortable. Since most people don't write stories as dialogue only, we suggest you write it in prose style as an outline to make sure you understand your story before you write the script.

Outline

Now that you've got your story mapped out, the next step is creating a detailed outline. Think of the outline as your North Star. If you get lost during the writing of the script, it will be your guide. An outline will help identify structural problems in your story lines and will show if the act break really works. The outline should show that the story works scene by scene and signifies that something is at stake. If you can take a scene out and the story still makes sense, then remove that scene. You should also include an arc (what a character does to accomplish a goal).

Also check the flow and pacing of scenes. Try to avoid using repetitive phrases or transition words like *meanwhile,* as it is not good form. At this stage you should also see if there's a continued escalation of the problem at hand. Make sure the conflict hits the wall in Act III.

From a writing standpoint, you need to make sure each act break poses dramatic questions. The stakes have to build so that the reader will care about what is going on with the characters and want to finish reading your entire script. Not only story stakes but emotional stakes need to be present as well. Ask yourself why each dramatic event is important to the main character.

If you consider skipping this step and diving right into writing your script (as we know many of you do), consider this quick reference list of the importance of the outline:

- It identifies structural problems in the story.
- It helps you see if the story works and make sure the story is advancing in every scene. (If you remove a scene and the story still works, then you know that scene isn't necessary.)
- It determines if your characters appear in each scene and helps check entrances and exits.
- It helps you ensure that the characters enter a scene with one attitude and leave with a slightly different one by the end of the scene.
- It determines if your act breaks work.
- It checks the flow and pacing of the stories.

We have included a sample from *Without a Trace* in chapter 9 of this book for your reference.

6.

Components of
a Drama Script

At the Workshop, we look for a variety of elements in a script, including the story idea(s), structure, character, and dialogue. Within those elements, we look at the setup, the act break, and the resolution, which are more technical terms. The best scripts score high in each of these areas, but most scripts fail in at least one, if not more. The following are the criteria we look for in each script.

Idea

Choosing a good idea(s) for each story line is key. Each story should be fresh and coherent. If the story feels like a story we've seen many times before, then you'll need to find a new way to tell it or come up with a different story. Your goal is to make the reader want to turn the page to find out what is happening next and, therefore, make your script memorable. Your talent is then based upon the execution of those ideas. Do they make sense? Do the various stories go together, and are they woven together thematically?

Story

Naturally, your story should be believable and credible. One of the first things professional readers look for is whether the first few pages of

40

the story and its conflict have been set up quickly enough. If a story takes too long to set up, readers lose interest. Also note if you have involved the lead character(s) as the focus of the story.

Whether you are writing an A-, B-, or C-story, each one must have a clear beginning, middle, and end. Every story has to be about something. Many scripts that we analyze have no actual story, because there's no conflict. Make sure your story makes sense.

The story's ending should be inevitable, yet surprising. The payoff should be satisfactory to the reader, so don't choose a story that is easily or can quickly be resolved. Don't have the conflict resolved by someone other than the main character(s).

Characters

Be sure to center the story lines on the show's main characters only and emphasize the characters and their feelings over the plot. In other words, keep the story simple, but allow the characters to be multidimensional and complex. Remember that procedural shows don't fall into this type of structure. No matter what show you are writing, be sure to show that you understand and can capture the voices of the show's main characters accurately. The characters should not just react to the problem or conflict but also drive the story by playing an active part in it.

Writing with emotion that demonstrates a character's feelings beneath a situation is a surefire way to get attention with your script. If the scenes are talky yet the story isn't advancing, there is definitely something wrong with the story. An important thing to consider here is that story *is* character. The story defines whom the character is by the way he or she behaves, which impacts the story and where it is going.

You also need to make sure that your story serves the characters as they are established in the actual show. In other words, don't change a character dramatically to serve your story. It will read as if you don't know the show. Always change your story to serve the character. Make sure you answer the obvious questions as to why the character just didn't do "this or that" to get out of his or her jam. Be on your character's side. *Show* what characters are feeling; don't just observe.

There sometimes is a tendency to focus on unknown characters, because it comes across as new or different. When you do introduce outside characters, make them interesting by giving them strong qualities or attitudes. This will give one or more of the major stars of the show something to react to and make the script more interesting. Also, you don't want to spend too much time introducing a new character when you may need those pages for your story.

An area writers tend to ignore is the entrances and exits of the characters. You need to give the characters a reason for coming and going within a scene. The reasons could be as simple as passing through one room to another or coming to get an item left in the room. You should also track your characters as they enter a scene thinking or feeling one way and wind up with a slightly different attitude by the end of that scene.

Dialogue

Make sure the dialogue reflects how the characters talk in the show and that the characters speak to each other. By the same token, make sure each line of dialogue advances the story. Start your scenes late and finish early.

Often, dialogue can read as contrived and forced. It may be riddled with one-liners that make it too choppy. Make sure the characters have motivation and a need for speaking. Another problem is repetitive dialogue, where a character repeats something in a variety of ways. It appears as though the writer can't think of what the character should say next.

Keep the characters' speeches short, no more than three or four lines unless it is a personality trait and is part of the show. Also, all characters who appear in a scene should have something to say; otherwise, don't bother to include them in the scene. If a character uses a certain catchphrase each week, make sure to include it.

Humor

On dramatic shows, there is usually at least one character who provides comic relief. If the show uses that character in a certain way, you should use that character the same way. Do not center your story on that person to be different.

Exposition

Exposition refers to the information that the reader must know in order to follow what is happening in the story. Expositional dialogue reveals information about the plot and the characters. If you find that a story suffers if expositional dialogue is removed, just make sure there isn't another place to put it. If plot and character information can be shown through images rather than dialogue, it would be beneficial, as it is better to *show* than to *tell*. Exposition should be worked into a story in small doses so that the story keeps moving. Scenes that have too much exposition lack conflict and drama.

Find a way to bring out exposition in an interesting way that doesn't get lost in long-winded speeches. Exposition can be inserted into dialogue through conflict, particularly when tempers flare and angry words are spoken.

Original voice

You should also incorporate your own voice. This is achieved from your choice of story or your point of view on a specific topic or issue. Just remember that you must not stray from the show's established boundaries.

The first draft

The first draft should be written quickly. Try not to be too critical at this stage, as it's too easy to get distracted. Even if a scene isn't working too well, try your best to keep writing. Then go back and rewrite and keep rewriting until you are completely satisfied. Remind yourself that you've laid down the foundation, because the structure is working. If you put aside an hour or two to work on your script on a given day, it's not unreasonable to expect to write two or three pages during that time.

The second draft and other rewrites

The way to write a better story, scene, or dialogue is to rewrite the material so it becomes more dramatic and entertaining. Although it's important to be able to write quickly, at this stage of the game, you can take as long as you need. Make corrections, clarify points, and make sure characters' emotions are intensified and dialogue is sharpened and tightened. Consider rewriting in stages, addressing one problem at a time. Go through your script and make notes in the margins.

Plug up holes in the story first, if necessary. If you've repeated a story point in two different scenes, determine which is stronger and eliminate the other. If the dialogue is running really long in each speech, you need to cut it down. This block of copy is known as a widow. Be critical and cut where you can to make the script tight.

During this stage, it's a good idea to again check all of the entrances and exits of each character. Also take another pass at jazzing up the stage directions to make the reading experience a visual one.

We hope that by now your story works, the voices are accurate, and everything else seems to be in order. We have created a list of hard-hitting questions you need to ask yourself prior to handing in your script to a television industry professional. If anything is amiss, go back to the script and fix it. Why send out a script if it isn't top-notch?

Story and structure questions

- Does your script contain the right amount of stories for the show that you are writing?
- Are the stories focused and well developed?

- Have you told a fresh story with a solid payoff, or is the story boring?
- Is the story logical?
- Does the main story begin early?
- Do any scenes lag?
- Is the dramatic conflict strong in each story line?
- Are the scenes built upon each other in a logical sequence of dramatic action?
- Do you have too many story lines?
- Does each scene reveal some kind of emotion?
- Are scenes overwrought with exposition?
- Are the scenes the right length?
- Are there enough twists and turns?
- Does anything happen that feels too convenient or obvious?
- Is the resolution too obvious, or is there a satisfying ending?
- Are any scenes repetitive?

Character questions

- Are every action and reaction justified? Is each character's motivation clear?
- Do the characters' attitudes track from scene to scene smoothly?
- Is there a reason for each character to be included in a scene?
- Do the characters have something to say if they are in a scene?
- Are the characters' voices accurate?
- Has the character revealed a variety of emotions?

Dialogue questions

- Is the dialogue too wordy or long?
- Do the characters sound like they do on the show?

Other noteworthy items

- Don't give actors directions on how to act.
- Avoid using exclamation points.
- Don't show off your knowledge of the show by throwing in little-known facts or back story.
- Be sure to describe the locations and visuals well.

Tips for a final check

If possible, consider conducting a table read of your script if you have some friends who are willing to read the characters for you. You can also just read it aloud yourself and tape it. Listening to the tape may present some problems that you would pick up on only if you heard the script aloud rather than just reading it over and over.

Polish

Proofread your script several times, and have someone else proof it too. There is no excuse for having spelling or grammatical errors. When a script is littered with mistakes, it leaves a negative impression on the reader. You want to come off as a seasoned pro, so after all of your hard work, spend some time rereading your script and correct those errors. We've even seen characters' names spelled incorrectly! Last words of advice: Don't let the script leave your hands until you are absolutely sure it is the best that you can do. Become a perfectionist if you aren't one already.

Formatting

When you begin writing the actual script, you want it to look as professional as possible, which means following an industry-standard format.

In general, on an hour-long show, there are roughly fifty-five to sixty pages that are divided into a teaser and four acts. The teaser is three or four pages, with one "riveting sequence." This usually takes place over the course of two scenes in an effort to get the viewer hooked. The first act is roughly fourteen to fifteen pages, the second act is about thirteen to fourteen pages, while the third and fourth acts are about twelve to thirteen pages each. Keep in mind that the act length varies from show to show depending on its structure. Scenes and acts can be longer or shorter—as each show has a unique format.

Looking professional

Scripts should be presented professionally. They should be printed on clean white three-hole-punched paper and then bound with two industry-standard brads (Acco brand no. 5 or no. 6), one in each of the first and third holes. If your local stationery store does not carry them, consider buying them on-line. Do not bind scripts in any other way or your script may be perceived as amateurish.

It is recommended that you obtain a produced script of the show, either through industry contacts if you have them or by purchasing a script book for that particular show. Each show has its own style, and you want to do your best in duplicating it. There should be a cover on the script that has the name of the show, the episode's title, the writer's name, and the writer's contact information. You do not need to include a cast list or any other production information.

There are plenty of terrific screenwriting software programs on the market, and they can easily be purchased at a few places where software is sold or on-line. Final Draft is one of the most popular and easy to use scriptwriting programs because it provides a ready-made format for nearly all current shows. There are several other scriptwriting programs on the market, so you may want to investigate and, if possible, talk to other writers to see what they use. There are plenty of free software demonstrations around the country at many computer stores. You can also check out the software manufacturers' Web sites for more details. If you can't find a sample script, there are TV formats available in standard screenplay books that are easy to follow.

You should also register your script on-line with the Writers Guild of America, which has two websites, http://www.wga.org for the west coast and http://wgaeast.org for the rest of the country. Or you can register with the U.S. Copyright Office (call 202–207–9100 to find out how) prior to sending your script to an industry contact.

Polishing Your Script

7.

My Script Is Finished— Now What?

So you have picked a series, come up with an appropriate story, done the research, and written a beat sheet, an outline, and a script. So you're done, right? Not quite. There are three major hurdles you have to clear. The first one is rewriting, the second is getting feedback, and the third is getting noticed.

The rewrite

Rewriting is something you will do for every script you write, even if you have the number-one show on television. Self-editing is considered to be one of the hardest skills to master, although it is crucial in your development as a writer. This is when you have to force yourself to take a step back and look at your script with an objective and unbiased eye. You have to be brutally honest with yourself and ask yourself these hard questions:

- Does the story really make sense?
- Does each scene advance the story?
- Do the characters feel forced in their dialogue or behavior?

- Is the story structure solid? Does it climax and resolve where it should?
- Did you start the story in the right place?
- For a comedy, are the jokes as good as they could be?
- For a drama, is the story compelling enough, and does it effectively mimic the tone of the show?

The next section may sound too obvious to mention, but so many people make the following mistakes we had to make sure to reiterate these points:

- Proofread, proofread, proofread. Make sure there are no spelling errors in your script.
- Punctuation. Make sure commas are in the right place.
- Make sure the characters' names are spelled correctly.
- Make sure your name is spelled correctly.
- Make sure there are no missing pages.

Feedback

In the television business, everybody has an opinion. As a writer, it is your job to listen to what people have to say about your script, then decide if listening to them is in the best interest of the material. This process is called notes. There is an art to taking notes. If you give your now finished masterpiece to your grandmother and she says she loves it, that's great. But unless your grandmother is running a network, it doesn't matter what she thinks. However, if you give your script to a prospective agent or employer and they have some ideas how to make your script stronger, listen to them. That's not to say they are always right, but how you take notes further defines you as a writer. Although you may not initially agree with some notes, accept them gracefully and consider them. If a few people feel the same way about a particular area, it's a good indication that something is amiss. If you are argumentative and stubborn about fixing something, you will never keep a job in this business. Be diplomatic. Be open-minded. And most important, be polite.

Getting noticed

Now that you have a perfectly polished script, you need to get it to people who can employ you. In the business world, you would blindly send your résumé directly to the company you want to work for. In the entertainment business, you need someone to send your "résumé" (script) in for you. Remember that if you send your script to a show, studio, or network, it will be thrown away unopened. This is for the company's protection. All of the studios have strict policies barring them from reading unsolicited material. In our Workshop, we do not accept any material without a signed release form stating that the writer has no recourse if they submit something that is similar to an idea already being explored at Warner Bros. Television. This means that scripts must come through a legitimate source, that is, a literary agent, which is the most common form of representation for writers. There are several well-known agencies that are constantly looking for fresh voices; however, getting their attention isn't always so easy.

Work in the industry

If a script is sent from outside California, the chances are slim to none that the envelope will even get opened. Again, as stated earlier, in order to be considered for a job in television (any job), you must be based in Los Angeles. Even though some shows are filmed elsewhere, the writing staffs and network and studio offices are in Los Angeles.

So once you move to LA, your chances of being taken seriously increase. Another good way to "get in the door" is to try to get a job in the television industry. There are so many jobs an entry-level person can do to start networking and find a way to get their script noticed. All of the studios and networks have on-line job postings, so finding out about employment opportunities is extremely easy.

Applying for the Warner Bros. Writers Workshop

Another option is applying to various workshops and fellowships. Many networks and studios have programs like this in place. The longest-running and most prestigious is the Warner Bros. Television Writers Workshop.

We encourage everyone who has written a script to apply if they are seriously interested in a TV writing career. The fee for initial submission is $30 for each drama script and $25 for each comedy script. If you are selected into either Workshop, the fee is $495 *per person*.

Please check out our Web site for the most updated information and applications or to ask questions (http://www.warnerbros.com/writersworkshop). If you don't have access to a computer, beginning on May 1 please leave your name and address on our hot line (1-818-954-7906) in order to receive the same information by mail. Don't forget to mention if you want to apply to the Comedy Workshop or the Drama Workshop.

Sample Outlines and Scripts

8.

Comedy Outline and Script

THE GEORGE LOPEZ SHOW
"Feel the Burn" Outline
By Luisa Leschin

COLD OPEN

INT. GEORGE AND ANGIE'S KITCHEN—NIGHT (NIGHT 1)

George and the family have just finished dinner. As Angie, Carmen, and Max clear away the plates, George watches Randy, Benny's boyfriend, wipe his plate clean with a piece of bread. George tells Randy he'll give him a loaf of bread and he can clean the whole kitchen. Randy says it's an honor to eat with Benny's family. Randy, "I spent all my life looking for the perfect woman and the whole time she was right under my nose, inspecting my parts."

Carmen notes it's funny how she likes older men and her grandmother likes younger men. Randy tells Carmen he has a younger brother. Carmen ignores him. Ernie explains if Randy married Benny and Carmen married

Randy's brother, Randy would be Carmen's step-grandfather and brother-in-law.

Randy reminds Benny if they want to catch the movie they want to see, they better leave. Benny says she's not feeling well and Randy should go without her. Ernie invites Randy to his house to watch *Amélie*. Randy says he's gonna wash his hair instead. As Randy leaves, Angie thanks him for the can of homemade cheese he brought. Randy says no problem, "my possible future step-mother-daughter-half-sister-" George cuts Randy off by slamming the door in his face. Angie asks George to throw out Randy's cheese. George says he's going to do with it what he does with the dog poop, "Put in it the scooper and launch it as far as I can." George exits to the backyard.

Benny crosses to the freezer, opens it, and fans herself with a bag of frozen peas. Angie asks what's wrong, and Benny says she's been burning up all day. Angie feels her forehead and comments it does feel hot and clammy. Benny, "And that's just the top half." Angie says this might be the beginning of menopause. Benny scoffs at the idea, and George reenters as Angie explains menopause isn't that big of a deal. "There's pills for the incontinence, hormone creams to restore lubrication . . ." Upon hearing this, George gags, then after a beat stops and says, "Hey, no vomit."

Angie tells George Benny should see a gynecologist. Benny says she doesn't want people to know about this. Benny, "I don't want them to think I'm less than a woman." George, "God forbid that secret gets out." Angie asks when Benny last saw a gynecologist. Benny answers it was when George was born. George and Angie react to Benny's cavalier attitude. Benny's rationale is, "When was the last time you called a plumber and they didn't find a leak?" to which Angie answers, "Oh, that's smart. It's better to wait for a pipe to burst and ruin your wood floors." George looks at Angie, who shrugs at the insanity of her analogy.

George tells Benny if there's something wrong with her, she should deal with it. He resolves to take her to the doctor, and Benny relents. George, "But I'm wearing headphones so I don't hear the gynecologist say, 'Oh my God! I quit!'"

FADE OUT.

END OF COLD OPEN

ACT ONE, SCENE A

INT. GEORGE AND ANGIE'S KITCHEN—THE NEXT DAY (DAY 2)

Angie's on the telephone as George and Benny enter from the living room. George, "Well, Mom and I are off to the gyno." Angie covers the mouthpiece and notes how dressed up Benny is. Benny, "I figure I'll feel less cheap if I have nice heels in the stirrups." George looks to Angie and repeats, "Well, Mom and I are off to the gyno."

RESET TO:

EXT. GEORGE AND ANGIE'S BACKYARD—CONTINUOUS

George and Benny enter the backyard, where Vic (Angie's father) is teaching Max to play the conga drums. George rhetorically asks how come one raft of horn players can't make it to Miami. George and Benny exit.

RESET TO:

INT. GEORGE AND ANGIE'S KITCHEN—CONTINUOUS

Back in the kitchen, Angie's still on the phone. Vic enters to hear Angie say, "Thank you, Mamí, you won't regret this." Angie hangs up, and Vic asks what her mother won't regret. Angie says she knows her mom was unfaithful, but she believes they can work out their differences if they see each other. Vic says there's nothing to work out. "It's over. It's done. It's deader than Castro's eyes." Angie asks Vic if her mother would be flying out from Miami tomorrow to see him if it was really over. After a beat, Vic agrees to see his estranged wife. Angie thanks Vic and hugs him. Vic, "It will be a pleasure to tell her to her face that she is a lying, cheating Jezebel who will burn in hell with her lover." Angie asks if he's been working on that for a while. Vic replies, "Getting mad in your second language isn't easy. Leave me alone," and walks out to the backyard.

DISSOLVE TO:

ACT ONE, SCENE B

INT. DOCTOR'S OFFICE WAITING ROOM—LATER THAT DAY (DAY 2)

George is sitting on a couch, waiting for Benny. He spots a man and an older woman sitting across the room and approaches them. George, to the man, "This is awkward, huh? I'm here with my mom too." The woman replies, "I'm his wife." George, "At least you don't have to worry about getting pregnant." Woman, "We've been trying for eleven years."

Benny enters the waiting room from the doctor's office. She looks shaken and takes a seat on the couch. George tells her she's taking this too hard; every woman goes through the change. "It's nothing to be ashamed of." Benny, "I've got the clap." George reacts and asks how this could happen. Benny, "Well, when a man and a woman love each other very much, and the man has a terrible disease in his pants . . ." George tells Benny she's old enough to be responsible and asks if Randy pressured her into doing something she was uncomfortable with. Benny, "Yeah, he told me it'd be okay—all the cool grandmas are doing it." George says this is why he didn't want her to date; she's too old. George, "You should be closing up the shop by now." Benny, "Well, the shop's still open, and now there's a cleanup on aisle two."

A nurse enters and tells Benny she didn't complete her medical history. Nurse, "Would you like to come back inside?" Benny, "No, let's do it here. The last time I went in there, you guys gave me the dripsies." The nurse tells Benny she didn't give her date of birth, and Benny scribbles it down. The nurse then asks, "And your second pregnancy. Did you carry it to full term?" Benny freezes. George asks Benny what the nurse is talking about. Benny, "You know what? I forgot to tell you—you have a sister." Benny then turns back to the nurse, asks to finish in the doctor's office, and quickly runs out to avoid George's incredulous reaction. On George's shocked expression, we:

FADE OUT.

END OF ACT ONE

ACT TWO, SCENE C
INT. GEORGE AND ANGIE'S KITCHEN—LATER THAT DAY (DAY 2)

Angie's at the kitchen island, going through some of her La Marie Cosmetics. George enters from the backyard with a head of steam. George, "You're not going to be believe this, Angie. I just found out my mother gave away a sister I never knew I had." Angie tries to stop him, but he continues. "It gets better. The only way I found out is because my mother has gonorrhea." Angie crosses to a customer who is standing by a mirror near the back door. "I'm helping Janet find a sunscreen for her trip to Mexico." George, "That's nice. Driving or flying?" Angie tells Janet to take the sunscreen, she'll bill her later, and escorts her out the back door. Angie then follows George into the backyard.

RESET TO:

EXT. GEORGE AND ANGIE'S BACKYARD—CONTINUOUS

Benny's sitting on the porch as Angie enters and asks what's going on. "First you have a father, now you have a sister?" Benny explains that after George's father left, she discovered she was two months pregnant. She already had a two year old and no money. "I did what I had to do." Benny says she made sure the baby went to a good family. George, "Why didn't you do that for me?" Benny crosses into the kitchen.

RESET TO:

INT. GEORGE AND ANGIE'S KITCHEN—CONTINUOUS

Benny enters, followed by George and Angie. George and Angie continue to ask Benny questions about her daughter, which Benny avoids answering. George asks if Benny remembers the name of the family who adopted her. Benny, "I think it was Mr. and Mrs. Mind-You-Own-Business-You're-Lucky-I-Kept-You . . . berg." George insists and Benny admits it was the Lorenzos who used to live down the street. George asks if the woman even knows she's adopted. Benny replies she doesn't know; the Lorenzos moved out of the neighborhood shortly after the adoption. George says he thinks he could find his sister. Benny tells him to stay out of it. "It's between me and your father." George asks if his father knows. Benny replies, "No. It's between me and me. Leave it alone," and exits.

George turns to Angie and says he can't leave it alone—what if his sister feels abandoned like he did

without a dad? Angie reminds George the sister might not
know she's adopted and he could shatter her whole world.
George, "Then I won't call her again." Angie says George
should have been old enough to remember his mom having a
baby. George says he recalls his mom getting fat and
remembers being sent to stay with the neighbors for a
couple weeks. Angie says that must have been very
traumatic for him. George says, "No. They had a puppy.
There was hugging. They taught me what breakfast was."
(Then, fondly) "Pancakes . . ."

DISSOLVE TO:

ACT TWO, SCENE D

INT. GEORGE AND ANGIE'S KITCHEN—THE NEXT MORNING (DAY 3)

Angie is working on the computer. George comes
downstairs and asks Angie what she's doing. She
explains she got up early and has been searching for
George's sister. She's cross-checked every Lorenzo in
California with the year the sister was born and has
narrowed it down to twenty possibilities. George says
he slept in, read the sports page, then called his old
neighbor and found out where the Lorenzos moved.
George, pointing to the screen, "It's that one." Angie
asks if he's called her yet. George says no. But he
found out her name is Linda and she works for the Valley
School District. He's going down to her office and meet
with her. Angie asks what he's going to say. George says
he's going to play it by ear, see if she knows she's
adopted, and go from there.

Vic enters and asks Angie if she can iron one of his
dress shirts. Angie observes he's going to dress up for
his reunion with Mom. Vic feigns disinterest, but Angie
calls him on it. Vic admits a marriage takes two people

and maybe he worked too hard, maybe he neglected her. Maybe he didn't tell her enough how beautiful she was, maybe he told her too much. George, "Maybe you annoyed her into another man's arms." Angie's excited for the reunion and says they're going to be a family again. Coupled with George meeting his sister for the first time, she notes, "Two families are coming together." Angie's suddenly overcome with emotion. George, "All right, then. I'll catch you later." He exits and Angie crosses to the sink to dab her eyes with a dishcloth. Benny enters from the living room and sees Angie. Benny, "What's the matter, princess? You gain half a pound?" Angie, "Benny, that hurts. But it doesn't burn." Angie exits, proud of her slam on Benny.

DISSOLVE TO:

ACT TWO, SCENE E
INT. LINDA LORENZO'S OFFICE—LATER THAT DAY (DAY 3)

Linda Lorenzo works at her desk. An assistant shows a nervous George into the office. He introduces himself and says he's from the Latino Association of Dyslexics. "L-A-D, I think. Right?" Linda asks George to have a seat.

Linda explains she usually doesn't take unscheduled meetings, but George's organization hits close to home—she's dyslexic herself. George says he is too and asks if it runs in her family. Linda says she knows it's usually genetic, but it's a mystery where hers came from. George, "Hmm . . . interesting." Linda asks George if he has brought any literature or brochures. George, caught, answers, "We at LAD try not to pressure ourselves with the written word."

George notices all the pictures on her desk. Linda

explains she's very close to her family. George picks one up. [Linda says,] "Oh, yes. I miss Cupcake so much. He was my childhood pony." George, "You had a pony?! I had to swim in a trash can!" Linda asks what she can do for George. George says, "Since we're both Latinos. . . ," but Linda cuts him off and says she's not Latina, she's Italian. George, laughing, "You think you're Italian?" Linda says her family is from Sicily, and they visit the island every year. They travel to a little church so her mother can pray to her patron saint for helping to conceive her. George, "So this Italian woman . . . she gave birth to you?" Linda, "Yes. That's why I call her Mom." Linda goes on to explain her parents gave her so much love and encouragement growing up; her mother even quit work to tutor her. She counts herself as very lucky.

George agrees and stands to leave. Linda, "What about LAD?" George, "Oh, forget about it. Let it go." George then surreptitiously takes a digital camera out of his pocket and snaps a photo of Linda. Linda asks what that was for. George, "It's for our dyslexia newsletter. It's all pictures." George gives Linda a big hug and holds her for a moment. George, "Take care of yourself. Watch your blood pressure." George exits quickly, leaving a confused Linda behind.

DISSOLVE TO:

ACT TWO, SCENE H

INT. GEORGE AND ANGIE'S KITCHEN—LATER THAT DAY (DAY 3)

Benny sits alone at the kitchen table. She takes a pill out of its container and swallows it. Randy enters and asks why Benny wasn't at work. Benny, "You disgusting piece of crap." Randy, "Oh, we're playing

that game? Alright, you dirty little garden gnome."
Benny says she's not playing a game, he gave her an STD,
and wants to know who he's been whoring around with.
Randy, "Just you, Benny. Just you." He goes on to say he
had no idea he was sick; he didn't have any symptoms.
Benny gives Randy a brochure and tells him he's going to
have to take two weeks of antibiotics. Randy says maybe
this is a blessing—since they can't have sex, maybe now
they can talk and really get to know each other. Benny
says he should call her after he's finished his meds and
burned the blanket in the back of his truck. Randy says
he's going to miss her, but Benny recoils and shouts,
"Back off, Outbreak!" She pushes Randy out the door and
closes it behind him.

Angie and Vic enter from upstairs. Vic is wearing a
suit and looks very dapper. Benny reacts to Vic's
overpowering cologne and says he's trying too hard; he
should put some of his cologne on a rag, hold it over
his wife's mouth, and drag her away. Vic agrees he
should air himself out in the backyard and exits.

George enters and Angie asks how it went with his
sister. Benny's surprised—she told him to leave it
alone. George says he met Linda, and she's very happy
and successful. George, to Benny, "Those two minutes
you had with her didn't ruin her." Angie asks when they
are going to meet her. George explains Linda doesn't
know she's adopted and he's not going to tell her. Benny
agrees with George's decision. George shows Angie the
picture he took of Linda. Angie, "Oh. She's got big
eyes." George, "I kinda surprised her with the camera."
George asks Benny if she wants to see the picture, but
she declines. George puts the picture down on the
counter and walks away.

The phone rings and Angie answers it. As she's talking on the phone, Benny crosses to the counter and takes a long look at the photo. George approaches Benny and puts his hand on her shoulder. They look at the photo together in silence.

Angie's phone conversation becomes heated. Angie, "You are being so selfish. How can you do this to Daddy?" After another beat Angie slams down the phone. Vic reenters from the backyard. Vic, "Somebody smell me." Angie can't bear to look at her father, and he asks what is wrong. Angie breaks the news to Vic: "Mom just called. She's not coming." Angie crosses to comfort her father, but Vic exits to the backyard.

Ernie enters with a blanket draped over his shoulders. Ernie, "Hey, look at the blanket Randy threw out. It's so warm and nice." As Ernie cuddles the blanket, we:

FADE OUT.

END OF ACT TWO

L.E.C.

EXT. GEORGE AND ANGIE'S BACKYARD—DAY (DAY 3)

George is playing Vic's congas. Vic enters and tells George he's doing it all wrong. Vic takes a seat next to George and tells him to listen and learn. Vic, "Don't play like you're killing a bug. Think of the congas as a woman, and then play them like you are making love to her." Vic plays a sensual rhythm and stops. George says he understands. George hits the conga once, hard, then stands. George, "I need a nap." As George exits, we:

FADE OUT.

END OF SHOW

The following script is the actual shooting draft of "Feel the Burn." We wanted to demonstrate how a story evolves from a comedy outline written in prose to a script written in dialogue. Please keep in mind that each show has its own style and format. We are showing you this one from *The George Lopez Show* strictly as an example.

"FEEL THE BURN"

Written by

Luisa Leschin

Directed by

John Pasquin

Production #176-354

AS BROADCAST
October 10, 2003

COLD OPEN

FADE IN:

INT. GEORGE AND ANGIE'S KITCHEN - NIGHT (NIGHT 1)
(George, Angie, Benny, Carmen, Max, Ernie, Randy)

(THE FAMILY AND RANDY, BENNY'S BOYFRIEND, ARE AT THE DINING
TABLE FINISHING DINNER. GEORGE WATCHES AS RANDY TAKES A
SMALL SCRAP OF BREAD AND RUNS IT OVER AND OVER HIS PLATE TO
CLEAN IT)

                         GEORGE

            Why don't I get you a loaf of bread

            and maybe you can clean the whole

            kitchen?

                         RANDY

            George, I am honored to sup with

            you. Who knew when I started

            working at the factory I'd be

            dating your mom?

(TURNING TO BENNY)

            I spent all my life looking for the

            perfect woman and the whole time

            she was right under my nose,

            inspecting my parts.

(BENNY AND RANDY GIGGLE)

                       RANDY (CONT'D)

(CHECKING HIS WATCH)

            Hey babe, if we're going to catch a

            movie, we'd better skedaddle.

                         BENNY

(WIPING HER FOREHEAD WITH HER NAPKIN)

          You know what? I don't feel so

          good. You better go on without me.

                         ERNIE

          I'll go to the movies with you.

          What were you going to go see?

                         RANDY

          Well, Benny was going to drag me to

          one of those Black-Guy-Kung-Fu-Guy

          buddy movies.

(LAUGHING)

          They never get along.

                         ERNIE

          Hey, you can come over to my house

          and watch "Superstars of

          Wrestling."

                         RANDY

          How can you watch that stuff? It's

          all fake.

                         ERNIE

(COVERING)

          I know.

                         RANDY

(GIVING BENNY A KISS)

          Good night, babe. Feel better.

                          ANGIE

          Oh, good night you guys. Randy,

          thanks again for the homemade

          cheese. I'll wash the coffee can

          out and I'll get it back to you.

                          RANDY

          No problem Angie.

(RANDY EXITS)

                          ANGIE

          Kids, go do your homework.

(CARMEN AND MAX EXIT UPSTAIRS. GEORGE GRABS THE COFFEE CAN)

                     ANGIE (CONT'D)

          George, are you going to throw that

          cheese in the trash?

                          GEORGE

          No. I'm going to do what I do with

          the dog poop. Put it in the

          scooper and launch it as far as I

          can.

(GEORGE EXITS TO THE YARD. BENNY GOES TO THE REFRIGERATOR,
OPENS THE FREEZER DOOR AND STARTS FANNING HERSELF)

                          ANGIE

          Benny, you okay?

                          BENNY

          I've been burning up all day.

(ANGIE GOES OVER TO BENNY AND FEELS HER FOREHEAD)

                    ANGIE

You do feel hot and clammy.

                    BENNY

And that's just the top half.

                    ANGIE

Do you have any other symptoms?

                    BENNY

Irritability.

                    ANGIE

Any new symptoms?

(BENNY PULLS OUT A BAG OF FROZEN VEGETABLES AND DABS HERSELF
WITH THE BAG)

                    BENNY

You know, female stuff.

                    ANGIE

Well Benny, you might be at that

age. This could be the beginning

of menopause.

                    BENNY

No, no, no. I just started dating

a forty-two year-old guy. I can't

be going through the change.

                    ANGIE

        Benny, it's not the end of the

        world.

(GEORGE RE-ENTERS, UNNOTICED BY ANGIE)

                    ANGIE (CONT'D)

        A gynecologist can help you.

        There's pills for the incontinence,

        hormone creams to restore

        lubrication...

(GEORGE CHOKES. THEN, SURPRISED)

                    GEORGE

        Hey, no vomit.

                    ANGIE

        Honey, I'm trying to talk your mom

        into seeing the doctor. She might

        be going through the change.

                    BENNY

        Hey, you don't have to tell

        everybody about this. I don't want

        people to think I'm less than a

        woman.

                    GEORGE

        Yeah, God forbid that secret gets

        out.

                    ANGIE

        When was the last time you saw your

        gynecologist?

                    BENNY

Oh, it's been a few years.

                    ANGIE

Well, how many years?

                    BENNY

Well, let's see, I was lying on my
back, full of drugs, George was
crying. So it was either the day
he was born, or Christmas 1973.

                    GEORGE

You haven't been to the doctor in
thirty-seven years? Cochina. You
should be ashamed of yourself.

                    BENNY

No, come on, they always find
something wrong with you. That's
how they make their money.

                    GEORGE

Look Mom, if there's problem,
you've got to deal with this, okay?
So you've gotta go to the doctor
tomorrow, even if I got to take
you.

                    BENNY

You are going to take me to the
gynecologist?

                        GEORGE

        Yeah, but I'm going to wear my

        headphones so I don't hear the

        gynecologist say, "Oh my God!   I

        quit!"

                                              FADE OUT.

                    END OF COLD OPEN

ACT ONE

SCENE A

FADE IN:

INT. GEORGE AND ANGIE'S KITCHEN/EXT. GEORGE AND ANGIE'S
BACKYARD - THE NEXT DAY (DAY 2)
(George, Angie, Benny, Max, Vic)

(ANGIE'S ON THE PHONE. GEORGE ENTERS WITH BENNY, WHO'S
DRESSED UP. VIC AND MAX ARE ON THE PATIO WITH CONGAS. VIC
PLAYS A BEAT)

                    GEORGE

          Well, Mom and I are off to the

          gyno.

                    ANGIE

(CUPPING THE PHONE, TO BENNY)

          Look at you. You're all dressed

          up.

                    BENNY

          Well, I figured I'd feel less cheap

          if I have some nice heels in the

          stirrups.

                    GEORGE

          Well, Mom and I are off to the

          gyno.

(GEORGE AND BENNY EXIT INTO THE YARD)

                                        RESET TO:

GEORGE LOPEZ "FEEL THE BURN"   AS BROADCAST   9.
    #176354   10/10/03   I/A

EXT. GEORGE AND ANGIE'S BACKYARD - CONTINUOUS

(VIC AND MAX ARE PLAYING CONGA DRUMS. GEORGE AND BENNY
CROSS INTO THE YARD)

                    GEORGE

            Hey Mambo Kings. Oye como va?

                    MAX

            Grandpa's teaching me the secrets

            of the conga.

                    VIC

            Listen to the heartbeat of Cuba.

(STARTING TO PLAY RHYTHMICALLY)

                Ca cong ca cong ca cucuye, Ca cong

                ca cong ca cucuye...

(MAX JOINS IN)

                    GEORGE

            Can't one raft of horn players make

            it to Miami?

(AS GEORGE AND BENNY EXIT, WE:)

                                                    RESET TO:

INT. GEORGE AND ANGIE'S KITCHEN - CONTINUOUS

(ANGIE IS STANDING BY THE ISLAND, TALKING ON THE PHONE WHEN
VIC ENTERS FROM THE YARD AND GOES TO THE FRIDGE)

                    ANGIE

(INTO PHONE)

                Thank you, Mom, you won't regret

                this.

(ANGIE HANGS UP AND NOTICES VIC)

                    VIC

What won't your mother regret?

                    ANGIE

Listen, Daddy, I know Mom was

unfaithful, but I think the two of

you can work this out if you can

just sit down in the same room

together.

                    VIC

No, mijita. There's nothing to

work out. It's over. It's done.

It's deader than Castro's eyes.

                    ANGIE

Daddy, if it were really over,

would she be flying here tomorrow

night to see you?

                    VIC

She's flying here?

                    ANGIE

Yes. So you'll talk to her?

                    VIC

Absolutely.

(ANGIE GIVES HER DAD A HUG)

                    ANGIE

Thank you, Daddy.

                              VIC

          It will be a pleasure to tell her

          to her face that she is a lying,

          cheating Jezebel who will burn in

          hell with her lover, boiling in a

          soup of their own treachery.

(AS VIC RETURNS TO THE CONGAS, MUTTERS IN SPANISH AND BEGINS
PLAYING AGAIN, WE:)

                                              DISSOLVE TO:

<u>SCENE B</u>

<u>INT. DOCTOR'S OFFICE WAITING ROOM - LATER THAT DAY (DAY 2)</u>
(George, Benny, Nurse, Woman, Man Extra, Extras)

(<u>GEORGE</u> HAS BEEN WAITING FOR A WHILE. HE FLIPS THROUGH A
MAGAZINE, THEN TOSSES IT BACK ONTO THE COFFEE TABLE.
GEORGE GLANCES OVER TO A <u>MAN</u> SITTING NEXT TO A <u>WOMAN</u> OLDER
THAN HIMSELF. GEORGE NODS AT THE MAN. THE MAN NODS BACK)

GEORGE

(TO THE GUY)

This is awkward, huh? I'm here

with my mom too.

WOMAN

I'm his wife.

GEORGE

Still awkward.

(GEORGE QUICKLY CROSSES AWAY. <u>BENNY ENTERS</u> THE WAITING
ROOM. SHE LOOKS SHAKEN AND SHE'S GOT A PAMPHLET FOLDED UP
IN HER HAND. GEORGE GOES TO HER)

GEORGE (CONT'D)

Mom, you alright?

BENNY

No, no, not really.

GEORGE

Come on, Mom, you're taking this too

hard. Every woman goes through the

change. It's nothing to be ashamed

of.

BENNY

George, I've got the clap.

                         GEORGE

What?! Mom, you're old enough to

be responsible. How could you let

this happen? Did Randy pressure

you into doing something you were

uncomfortable with?

                         BENNY

Yeah, he did. He told me that it

would be okay, and that all the

cool grandmas are doing it.

(THEN)

I'm going to kill him for giving me

this.

                         GEORGE

This is why I didn't want you to

date. Mom, you're too old. You

should be closing up the shop by

now.

                         BENNY

Well, the shop is still open and

now there's a clean up in aisle

two.

(A NURSE ENTERS)

                         NURSE

Mrs. Lopez?

                         BENNY

What?

                          NURSE

          I'm sorry, but you didn't complete

          some of the questions on your

          medical record. Would you like to

          come back inside?

                          BENNY

          No, let's do it out here. The last

          time I went in there, you guys gave

          me the dripsies.

                          NURSE

          Let's see, your birth date-- you

          only wrote a four.

                          BENNY

          Gimme that.

(BENNY TAKES THE CLIPBOARD, SCRIBBLES THE DATE AND PUSHES IT
BACK TO THE NURSE)

                          NURSE

          Okay. And your second pregnancy.

          Now did you carry that to full

          term?

(BENNY FREEZES)

                          GEORGE

          Second pregnancy? Mom, what the

          hell is she talking about?

(BENNY SWALLOWS HARD)

                          BENNY

          You know what? I forgot to tell

          you, you have a sister.

(THEN, TO THE NURSE)

          Let's finish this inside.

(AS BENNY EXITS INTO THE DOCTOR'S AREA, WE:)

                                              FADE OUT.

                    END OF ACT ONE

ACT TWO

SCENE C

FADE IN:

INT. GEORGE AND ANGIE'S KITCHEN/EXT. GEORGE AND ANGIE'S
BACKYARD - LATER THAT DAY (DAY 2)
(George, Angie, Benny, Customer Extra)

(ANGIE IS AT THE COUNTER WITH HER LA MARIE COSMETICS SALES
CASE OPEN. GEORGE ENTERS FROM THE YARD AND CROSSES RIGHT
TO HER)

                    GEORGE

        You're not going to believe this,

        Angie. I just found out my mom

        gave away a sister I never knew

        that I had.

                    ANGIE

        George...

                    GEORGE

        No, wait. It gets better. And the

        only way that I found out is

        because my mom has gonorrhea.

                    ANGIE

        George,

(ANGIE CROSSES TO A WOMAN WHO IS STANDING AT THE MIRROR BY
THE BACK DOOR)

                    ANGIE (CONT'D)

        this is Janet. She's a customer.

        I'm showing her sunscreens because

        she's taking a lovely trip to

        Mexico.

                              GEORGE

(TO JANET)

          Hey, how would you feel about

          taking an itchy old lady with you?

                              ANGIE

(GATHERING UP JANET'S THINGS)

          Just take the sunscreens. I'll

          bill you later.

(ANGIE SHOWS JANET OUT THE BACK DOOR. ANGIE FOLLOWS GEORGE
AS HE EXITS TO THE YARD)

                                               RESET TO:

EXT. GEORGE AND ANGIE'S BACKYARD - CONTINUOUS

                              ANGIE

          What is going on?! First you have

          a father, and now you have a

          sister?

(THEN, TO BENNY)

          How many family members are you

          hiding from him?

                              BENNY

          You know what, don't judge me.

          After Manny walked out on us, then

          I found out I was pregnant. I

          already had a two year-old and no

          money. I did what I had to do.

                         GEORGE

So you gave up my sister just like

that?

                         BENNY

I made sure she went to a good

family.

                         GEORGE

Why didn't you do that for me?

(BENNY GRABS HER PILLS AND EXITS TO THE KITCHEN)

                                              RESET TO:

INT. GEORGE AND ANGIE'S KITCHEN - CONTINUOUS

(BENNY ENTERS FOLLOWED BY GEORGE AND ANGIE)

                         ANGIE

Benny, have you stayed in touch

with her? Does she even know about

us?

                         BENNY

Oh crap, here we go.

                         GEORGE

Mom, this is my sister. I want to

know about her. What's the name of

the family that adopted her?

                         BENNY

Let's see, wait, wait, it was

Mister and Missus Mind-Your-Own-

Business-You're-Lucky-I-Kept-You...

Berg.

                        GEORGE

        Names, Mom.

                        BENNY

        Oh, for God's sake. It was the

        Lorenzos, you 'member, they used to

        live down the street.

                        GEORGE

        Does she know that she's adopted?

                        BENNY

        How the hell should I know? They

        moved out of the neighborhood.

                        GEORGE

(TO ANGIE)

        I bet I could find them.

                        BENNY

        No. Hey, you know what? You stay

        out of this. It's between me and

        your father.

                        GEORGE

        So Manny knows about this?

                        BENNY

        No. It's between me and me. Leave

        it alone.

(BENNY EXITS. GEORGE WATCHES HER GO)

                    GEORGE

Leave it alone? Ta loca, leave it

alone.

                              DISSOLVE TO:

SCENE D

INT. GEORGE AND ANGIE'S KITCHEN - THE NEXT MORNING (DAY 3)
(George, Angie, Benny, Vic)

(ANGIE IS AT THE COMPUTER, SEARCHING FOR GEORGE'S SISTER.
GEORGE ENTERS FROM UPSTAIRS WITH THE CORDLESS PHONE)

                    GEORGE

(INTO PHONE)

          Alright, well thanks a lot. I

          appreciate it. Uh huh. Bye.

(GEORGE HANGS UP AND CROSSES TO ANGIE)

                    GEORGE (CONT'D)

          What are you doing?

                    ANGIE

          I got up early. I've been on the

          computer for hours searching for

          your sister. I've cross-checked

          every Lorenzo in California with

          the year your sister would have

          been born and I've narrowed it down

          to twenty.

                    GEORGE

          Well I slept in, took a long

          shower, read the sports page, then

          I called my mom's neighbor and

          found out where the Lorenzos moved.

(OFF THE COMPUTER SCREEN)

          It's that one right there.

                    (MORE)

                    GEORGE (CONT'D)
       But look at you, surfing the web.

       You rock.

                      ANGIE
       Did you call her?

(GEORGE GETS OUT THE DIGITAL CAMERA AND LOADS SOME BATTERIES
  INTO IT)

                      GEORGE
       Well not yet. I found out she

       works for the Valley School

       District. When her office opens,

       I'm gonna go down and meet her.

                      ANGIE
       What are you going to say to her?

                      GEORGE
       I'm gonna play it by ear. I mean,

       I've got to figure out whether she

       knows she's adopted, then I'll take

       it from there.

(THEN)

       But her name's Linda. "Hey, give

       me five bucks, I'll let you watch

       my sister Linda change." That

       sounds nice, huh?

(VIC ENTERS, WEARING A ROBE AND HOLDING A DRESS SHIRT)

                          VIC

(TO ANGIE)

            Oye mijita, can you iron this

            shirt?

                          ANGIE

(TAKING THE SHIRT)

            Sure, Daddy.

(THEN, NOTICING)

            Did you trim your eyebrows?

                          VIC

            Just one. I put an arch in it. It

            makes me look interested when

            people are talking, as if I'm

            saying, "Is that so?"

                          ANGIE

            You're gonna dress up for Mom

            tonight, aren't you?

                          VIC

            That's tonight? I completely

            forgot about it.

                          ANGIE

            Daddy, I know when you're lying.

VIC

(POINTING HIS ARCHED EYEBROW AT HER)

     Is that so?

(THEN, OFF HER LOOK)

     Alright, mi niña. I was rehearsing

how I was going to tell her off,

but then I got to thinking. A

marriage takes two people. Maybe I

worked too much. Maybe I neglected

her. Maybe I didn't tell her

enough how beautiful she was or

maybe I told her too much.

GEORGE

(UNDER HIS BREATH)

     Maybe you annoyed her into another

man's arms.

ANGIE

I have a good feeling about this,

Daddy. We are going to be a family

again.

(SHE HUGS HIM)

     And George, he's going to meet his

sister for the first time in thirty

five years. This is so beautiful.

My mom, my dad. You, your sister.

(TEARING UP)

     Two families are coming together.

GEORGE

(PATTING HER ON THE SHOULDER)

Alright, I'll catch you later.

(GEORGE EXITS. ANGIE CROSSES TO THE ISLAND AND GRABS A DISH
TOWEL. BENNY ENTERS FROM THE LIVING ROOM AND SEES ANGIE
WIPE HER EYES)

BENNY

Oh, what's the matter, princess?

You gain half a pound?

ANGIE

Benny, that hurts. But it doesn't

burn.

(AS ANGIE EXITS, WE:)

DISSOLVE TO:

SCENE E

INT. LINDA LORENZO'S OFFICE - LATER THAT DAY (DAY 3)
(George, Linda, Assistant Extra)

(LINDA IS NEAR HER DESK IN HER WELL-APPOINTED OFFICE)

SFX: THERE'S A KNOCK ON THE DOOR

                    LINDA

      Come in.

(AN ASSISTANT OPENS THE DOOR AND SHOWS GEORGE IN)

                    GEORGE

      Linda Lorenzo?

                    LINDA

(LOOKING UP)

      Yes.   George Lopez?

                    GEORGE

      We spoke on the phone. I'm with

      the Latino Association of

      Dyslexics. L-A-D, I think. Right?

                    LINDA

      Have a seat.

(GEORGE SITS DOWN AND LOOKS AT HER FOR A LONG BEAT)

                    GEORGE

      Look at you. Linda Lorenzo.

      I can't believe I'm actually face

      to face with my own...

      Superintendent of the Valley School

      District.

                         LINDA

           I normally don't take unscheduled

           meetings but your cause hits close

           to home because I'm dyslexic.

                         GEORGE

           You know, me too. It must run in

           your family, right?

                         LINDA

           Actually not. I know it's usually

           genetic, but it's kind of a mystery

           where mine came from.

                         GEORGE

           Huh.   Interesting.

(THEN, OFF SOME FAMILY PICTURES ON HER DESK)

           You got a lot of pictures of your

           family.

                         LINDA

           Yeah, we're very close.

                         GEORGE

(THEN, OFF A PHOTO OF A YOUNG LINDA AND A PONY)

           Wow, that's a nice one.

                         LINDA

           Oh, yes. I miss Cupcake so much.

           He was my childhood pony.

                         GEORGE

           You had a pony?! I had to swim in

           a trash can!

> LINDA

What?

> GEORGE

Oh, I'm sorry, Gulf War.

> LINDA

Mr. Lopez, what can I do for your
organization?

> GEORGE

Well, I thought that since we're
both Latinos, and this is an issue-

> LINDA

(LAUGHING)

Oh, actually, I'm not Latina, I'm
Italian. But I get that all the
time.

> GEORGE

(LAUGHING)

You think you're Italian?

> LINDA

I don't think I'm Italian. I am
Italian. *Siciliana.* We visit
Sicily every year. We go to this
little church where my mother prays
to her patron saint for helping to
conceive me.

                              GEORGE

...So this Italian woman, she gave

birth to you?

                              LINDA

Yes. That's why I call her Mom.

                              GEORGE

See, the reason I ask is that a lot

of dyslexic kids had unhappy

childhoods. Did you ever wish that

you had different parents?

                              LINDA

Never. My parents gave me so much

love and encouragement. My mom

even quit work to tutor me. I'm

really lucky.

                              GEORGE

Yeah, you are.

(HE STANDS UP TO LEAVE)

Well, I think I've taken enough of

your time.

                              LINDA

But what about LAD?

                              GEORGE

Forget about it. Let it go.

(GEORGE PULLS OUT A DIGITAL CAMERA FROM HIS POCKET AND TAKES
A PICTURE OF LINDA, SURPRISING HER)

                        LINDA

    What was that?

                        GEORGE

    Oh, it's for our dyslexia

    newsletter. It's all pictures.

(GEORGE STARTS TO LEAVE)

                        GEORGE (CONT'D)

(FIGHTING BACK THE EMOTION)

    You take care of yourself.

(GIVING HER A HUG)

    And watch your blood pressure.

(GEORGE EXITS QUICKLY. OFF LINDA'S CONFUSED REACTION, WE:)

                                        DISSOLVE TO:

GEORGE LOPEZ   "FEEL THE BURN"   AS BROADCAST   31.
    #176354   10/10/03   II/H

SCENE H

INT. GEORGE AND ANGIE'S KITCHEN - LATER THAT DAY (DAY 3)
(George, Angie, Benny, Ernie, Vic, Randy)

(BENNY IS ALONE IN THE KITCHEN. SHE PICKS UP A GLASS OF
WATER AND SWALLOWS ONE OF HER ANTIBIOTICS. THEN, SHE OPENS
A CAN OF BEER, POURS IT INTO A GLASS AND CLOSES HER EYES AS
SHE TAKES A LONGING WHIFF. THERE'S A KNOCK AT THE DOOR.
RANDY LETS HIMSELF IN)

                    RANDY

I got your message. Why aren't you

at work today, baby doll?

                    BENNY

You disgusting piece of crap.

                    RANDY

Oh, we're playing that game?

Alright, you dirty little garden

gnome.

                    BENNY

Hey, you idiot. You gave me an

S.T.D.

                    RANDY

What are you talking about?

                    BENNY

You gave me the clap. Now, who

have you been whoring around with,

huh?

                         RANDY

        Just you, Benny, just you.

(BENNY GIVES HIM A SKEPTICAL LOOK)

                    RANDY (CONT'D)

        You're the best thing that ever

        happened to me. Why would I do

        anything to mess that up? I swear

        I didn't know I had it.

                         BENNY

        Well the tramp you were with before

        me must've given you a little going

        away present.

                         RANDY

(MOVING TO HUG HER)

        Benny, I'm so sorry.

                         BENNY

(SLAPPING HIS HANDS AWAY)

        Just tell it to the clinic. You're

        going to be taking penicillin for

        two weeks.

(BENNY OPENS THE DOOR FOR RANDY TO LEAVE)

                         RANDY

        Well maybe this is a blessing. I

        mean, we can just talk and get to

        know each other and really open up.

                              BENNY

          Right. Or maybe you can call me

          after you've finished your meds and

          burned the blanket in the back of

          your truck.

                              RANDY

(GOING TO HUG HER)

          I'm going to miss you, baby.

                              BENNY

(SLAPPING HIS HANDS AWAY)

          Back off, Outbreak.

(BENNY PUSHES RANDY OUT THE DOOR AND SHUTS IT. ANGIE AND
VIC COME DOWNSTAIRS. VIC IS WEARING A SUIT)

                              ANGIE

          Daddy, you look great. I don't

          think Mommy's going to be able to

          resist you.

                              BENNY

(WAVING A HAND IN FRONT OF HER NOSE)

          Whoa. I think you're taking this a

          little too seriously, Vic. Why

          don't you take some of that cologne

          and put it on a rag, pop it over

          her mouth and drag her away, huh?

VIC

Perhaps I should air myself out in

the backyard.

(AS VIC EXITS TO THE BACKYARD, HE PASSES GEORGE, WHO IS
CROSSING INSIDE. GEORGE MAKES A FACE AND COVERS HIS MOUTH
AND NOSE)

GEORGE

Hey, no vomit.

ANGIE

Honey, what happened? Did you meet

your sister?

BENNY

What? I told you to leave it

alone.

GEORGE

Well, I didn't. And I met her.

And she's very happy and she's very

successful.

(TO BENNY)

So I guess those two minutes she

spent with you didn't ruin her.

ANGIE

When are we gonna meet her?

GEORGE

We're not. She doesn't know she's

adopted, Angie, and I'm not going

to tell her.

                         BENNY

          Good.

                        GEORGE

          I took a picture of her though.

(GEORGE PULLS OUT HIS CAMERA AND SHOWS ANGIE)

                         ANGIE

          Oh. She's got big eyes.

                        GEORGE

          Well, I kinda surprised her with

          the camera.

(THEN)

          Mom, you want to see?

                         BENNY

          No.

(GEORGE CAREFULLY PLACES THE CAMERA ON THE ISLAND AND EXITS
UPSTAIRS)

SFX: PHONE RINGS

                         ANGIE

          I got it.

(ANGIE GOES TO ANSWER THE PHONE)

                    ANGIE (CONT'D)

          Hello? Hi.

(GEORGE COMES BACK DOWNSTAIRS. HE SEES BENNY CROSS TO THE
CAMERA, PICK IT UP AND LOOK LONG AND HARD AT THE PHOTO)

                         BENNY

          Huh.

(GEORGE CROSSES TO BENNY AND PUTS HIS HAND ON HER SHOULDER.
ANGLE ON: ANGIE, TALKING ON THE PHONE)

                            ANGIE

        You are being so selfish. How can

        you do this to Daddy? And to

        me?... No, I don't understand and

        I don't want to understand.

(ANGIE SLAMS THE PHONE DOWN. VIC ENTERS FROM THE BACKYARD
AND CROSSES TO ANGIE, HIS ARMS STILL IN THE AIR FROM AIRING
HIMSELF OUT)

                            VIC

        Someone smell me.

(ANGIE CAN'T BEAR TO LOOK AT HER FATHER)

                        VIC (CONT'D)

        What is it?

                            ANGIE

        Mom just called. She's not coming.

(BEAT)

                            VIC

        Huh.

(ANGIE GOES OVER TO COMFORT HIM. HE GENTLY WAVES HER OFF
AND SILENTLY CROSSES OUTSIDE. ERNIE ENTERS, CARRYING A
BLANKET)

                            ERNIE

        Hey guys, look at the blanket Randy

        threw out.

(AS THEY LOOK AT HIM, WE:)

                                            FADE OUT.

                    END OF ACT TWO

GEORGE LOPEZ   "FEEL THE BURN"   AS BROADCAST   37.
    #176354   10/10/03   L.E.C.

<u>L.E.C</u>

<u>FADE IN:</u>

<u>EXT. GEORGE AND ANGIE'S BACKYARD - DAY (DAY 3)</u>
(George, Vic)

(<u>GEORGE</u> IS PLAYING THE CONGAS WHEN <u>VIC ENTERS</u>. VIC SHAKES
HIS HEAD AT HOW GEORGE IS PLAYING)

                         VIC

         Hey, hey, hey, hey, hey. You are

         doing it all wrong.

(VIC SITS DOWN NEXT TO GEORGE)

                         VIC (CONT'D)

         Listen and learn. Don't play it

         like you're killing a bug. Think

         of the congas as a woman and then

         play them like you're making love

         to her.

(VIC PLAYS A SENSUAL RHYTHM AND STOPS)

                         GEORGE

         I got it.

(GEORGE HITS THE CONGA WITH ONE HAND AND GETS UP. AS HE
 EXITS, WE:)

                                              <u>FADE OUT.</u>

                     <u>END OF SHOW</u>

9.

Drama Outline and Script

WITHOUT A TRACE
"Birthday Boy" Outline
Episode 1
By Hank Steinberg

TEASER

1. SWEEPING SHOTS OF MANHATTAN—6 PM Friday. Tons of traffic. People jammed on the streets, leaving work at the end of a long day. MAKE our way DOWN to the D-Train SUBWAY stop at 86th Street and Broadway . . .

2. INT. SUBWAY PLATFORM—86TH STREET—40ish BOB FELDMAN descends the staircase with his eleven-year-old son, GABE. Father (wearing full Yankee regalia) and son (dressed a bit more hip, wearing a distinctive "Thrasher" jacket and a Yankee cap) headed for the Yankee game. Father excitedly hands one ticket to son, keeping the other for himself. They move toward the turnstile. Father hands son his Metro card. Son swipes it, goes through turnstile, hands Metro card back to

Father. Father swipes it once, then twice, then realizes the card is tapped. Father and son now separated by turnstile, Son on the platform, Father forced to retreat to the ticket booth to renew his Metro card. Father tells Son to stay put, but Father gets caught in line. The train comes. Son beckons Father to hurry. Train doors open. Son boards train. Father moves through turnstile, but his sweater gets caught. Son rolls his eyes. A rush of people push Son farther back into the train. Doors begin to close. Father extricates his sweater, rushes toward the subway, too late. He screams something to his son. Their faces separated by the window of the subway, they can see each other but can't begin to hear. The subway moves down the track, Father running alongside it, yelling to his Son who then fades away, the subway rumbling into the dark tunnel . . .

3. EXT. YANKEE STADIUM—9 AM THE FOLLOWING DAY—The D Train, now aboveground, rumbles into the 161st Street Station at the stadium. We BOOM DOWN to the stadium, where a handful of Yankee employees prepare for the day game, which begins in a few hours. Here we FIND Bob Feldman's wife DALE taping "Missing" posters with Gabe's picture to every pole they can find. Police are here, too. And some news crews, reporting on the disappearance of the "Birthday Boy" (DOD was Gabe's eleventh birthday). Bob tells JACK and SAMANTHA the story of what happened after they got separated at 86th Street: Bob got on the next train, got off at the next stop (96th Street). That's what he was screaming at Gabe through the window, but doesn't know if Gabe heard him. When Gabe wasn't there, he figured Gabe would meet him at

the game, so he jumped on the next train and headed up
to the stadium. He didn't see him on the platform there,
didn't find him at Gate 4, so he went to the game,
thinking Gabe was probably in his seat. When Gabe wasn't
there he started to freak out, and that's when he went
to the police. Dale comes over to Jack, distraught, but
feeling optimistic because the Yankees are being so
helpful to them; someone must have seen something. Jack
reassures her that they're going to do everything in
their power. But when he and Samantha walk off and have
a private moment alone, Samantha says. "We don't even
know if the kid ever made it here." Jack looks around
the vast expanse outside Yankee Stadium, now relatively
empty but soon to be mobbed, and says sarcastically:
"Even if he did, last night was perfect weather and the
Red Sox. There were fifty thousand people here
yesterday." And from Jacks POV, a crowd appears; our
missing boy could be anywhere. "Who's going to notice an
eleven-year-old kid by himself?"

ACT ONE

1. INT. FBI—Team debriefing. Gabe's picture goes up on
the board. Establish TIME LINE—Gabe got on subway at
6:05 P.M, and after that, we know nothing. It's now
10:15 A.M, and he's been missing for sixteen hours.
VIVIAN will coordinate the effort at Yankee Stadium.
Samantha's begun research on convicted child
abusers/pedophiles who live in the vicinity of the D
line (concentrating on those living above 86th Street).
Jack wants to know if they've found any witnesses
(anyone on the track yesterday) who can corroborate the
Father's story. Not yet. But DANNY'S monitoring the
subway stops with the NYPD, to see if the kid was

spotted anywhere on the D line from Manhattan to the
Bronx. Jack assigns MARTIN to the office to field all
incoming calls to "Gabe sightings" (now that the kid's
in the news). Most will inevitably be bogus, but they
all have to be considered and/or run down. (There is a
subtext here that Martin got this assignment because he
is still in the doghouse.) Then Jack's got a polygraph
appointment with the father: if the father wanted to do
something to this kid, getting him lost this way would
be awfully convenient.

2. INT. FELDMAN APARTMENT—Modest three-bedroom on Upper
West Side. Bob's a teacher; his wife, Dale, is a nurse.
Jack gives reluctant Bob a polygraph: running him
through the events of that day, the mixup at the
subway . . .

**3. FLASHBACK—EXT. 86TH STREET—Bob and Gabe head toward
the subway entrance. Bob is going on and on how great
it's going to be. Gabe is a bit blasé, doesn't think
it's that big a deal. Bob says, "What are you talking
about?" Yanks vs. Red Sox—when he was a kid he would
have killed for his dad to take him to a game. Bob hands
Gabe his ticket . . .**

4. RESUME in FELDMAN APARTMENT—Jack wants to know why
Bob gave him his own ticket, why he didn't hold onto
both tickets. Bob says, "It was Gabe's birthday. He's
eleven. I just thought he was old enough to hold his own
ticket." Jack wants to know if everything in the family
is okay. Bob replies, "Yes, absolutely." Any problems
with Gabe at school? "No." Any problems at home? "No."
Was Gabe angry about anything? "No." Did he ever play

hooky from school? "No." As Jack questions, Bob gets frustrated and angry. "This was a mixup on the subway, and you're wasting time questioning me when whoever has my son is out there!"

5. INT. SUBWAY PLATFORM—86TH STREET—Danny trying to find witnesses who may have seen the boy, showing Gabe's and Bob's pictures to beggars and musicians who frequent the area. Talking to people in Yankee outfits on their way to today's game—maybe these diehards went yesterday, too.

6. EXT. YANKEE STADIUM—Vivian talks to VENDORS and USHERS to see if they recognize Gabe's picture. (They have a picture of the distinctive jacket he was wearing yesterday.) So far, no luck . . .

7. INT. FBI OFFICE—Martin fields calls on "Gabe sightings." Puts pins into a map of New York City. They're accumulating—most of them are false leads that have to be run down by the NYPD.

8. EXT. HARLEM APARTMENT—Samantha and the local NYPD, following a lead from a neighbor, prepare to bust in on a convicted "reformed" pedophile who was seen yesterday with a boy matching Gabe's description.

9. INT. HARLEM APARTMENT—They bust down the door to find the PEDOPHILE sitting on his couch, alone, looking perplexed. He cries out to them, "What are you doing here?" They bark, "Where's the boy?" He says, "What are you talking about? I'm clean. I'm reformed. I've been to counseling." They move into the apartment, charging

into his bedroom where they find a wall covered with magazine cutouts of eight- to twelve-year-old boys. But no sign of Gabe . . .

10. INT. SUBWAY—154TH STREET—Danny finds an aging African American VIOLINIST who plays the subways for money, who *did* see Gabe yesterday . . . and Gabe appears before our eyes . . .

11. FLASHBACK—6:30 PM YESTERDAY—Gabe approaches the violinist, trying to figure out how to get to Yankee Stadium. He thought this was the stop. The violinist tells him he got off one too early; it's the next one. Gabe thanks him and gives him a dollar. The violinist notes Gabe's distinctive jacket and says he likes it. Gabe smiles, flattered, and thanks him. Gabe seems the picture of innocence . . .

12. RESUME SUBWAY—154TH STREET—Violinist tells Danny that he talked to Gabe for a few minutes, Gabe didn't mention his dad, didn't seem lost or worried, then got on the next train for Yankee Stadium. And that was that.

13. TIMELINE SHOT: 6:30 PM—Gabe gets off subway at 154th Street. 6:35 PM—Gets back on, heading uptown.

14. INT. YANKEE OFFICES—Vivian with Yankee Stadium employees. They found Gabe's ticket stub. Apparently, he did go to the game. But why didn't he make it to his seat? Vivian replies: "It may not have been Gabe who used the ticket. The seat next to this one—they're season tickets, right? Can we get their names?"

15. INT. GABE'S ROOM—Jack looks through Gabe's possessions, posters on his wall, his clothes, a skateboard. Trying to get a sense of this kid. Gabe's ghost appears to Jack. Dale comes in, apologizes for Bob. Knows that Jack is doing what he has to do. She says she's heard that if they don't find a child within 48 hours that he's probably . . . She can't say the words. Jack tries to reassure her. She asks if he has a child. He does, a son. She asks his name. They share a moment. His cell phone rings. Vivian briefs him as Dale looks on, seeing a change in Jack's expression, realizing there's news. Jack hangs up the phone, tells her what they know. Turns out some guy showed up in the third inning with Gabe's ticket, after Bob had already come and gone. The people in the seats next to Gabe's asked the guy where he got the ticket. He said he bought it from a scalper. Dale panics, thinking those scalpers are dangerous. "Aren't they?" Jack assures her they will find him.

16. EXT. CENTRAL PARK—BOATHOUSE—The guy who rents the boats at the boathouse is the one who bought the ticket off the scalper. (He struck up a conversation with the people sitting next to him—the season ticket holders— and told them what he did for a living, and that's how we found him.) Samantha shows the BOATHOUSE GUY pictures of various scalpers that work at Yankee Stadium. Boathouse guy IDs the scalper.

17. EXT. YANKEE STADIUM—Jack, Danny, Samantha, and Vivian all here now, scouring the stadium for the scalper. The scalper they are after has a serious

record—did time for armed robbery. They find him in a corner, wheeling and dealing, and move in. He runs. They chase, throw him to the ground. Got him.

ACT TWO

1. INT. FBI OFFICE—Jack and Vivian interrogate SCALPER, who swears up and down he has no idea what happened to Gabe. They show him Gabe's picture. Yeah, he remembers the kid . . .

2. FLASHBACK—Scalper making a deal with CUSTOMERS. Gabe comes over, wanting to sell his ticket. Scalper wants to see it. Gabe won't let him touch the ticket. Scalper laughs, comments that Gabe is a "smart little cracker" (and we see a savviness in Gabe we haven't seen before). They negotiate a deal, scalper giving him a hard time on the price because it is a single ticket, Gabe arguing that it's the Red Sox and it's a sellout. They settle on a price, Gabe hands him the ticket, the scalper hands him the money . . .

3. RESUME IN FBI INTERROGATION ROOM—Scalper tells us he liked the kid; he was smart and tough. Scalper: "Yeah, I've got a record, but I ain't no molester. When I was inside I'd be the first one in line to beat up those scum." The scalper says there are a half-dozen other scalpers who witnessed the transaction and can back up his story.

4. INT. FBI OFFICE—The scalper's story has checked out. Thus, armed with this new information that Gabe did, in fact, make it to Yankee Stadium and sold his ticket, why would he do it? (They've contacted the parents, and they

have no idea.) They discuss: eleven-year-old kid, not
particularly into baseball, took the opportunity to
bolt and go meet his friends? A girlfriend? Do drugs?
Guess this kid wasn't as innocent as his parents
thought, but he has never been so rebellious as to not
come home. So wherever he went, something must have
happened to him. Or could he possibly have run away?
It's time to pour all their energy into finding out
everything they can about him—that's the only way
they'll find out where he might have gone from Yankee
Stadium. Danny's assigned to check out all of Gabe's
Internet activity, Vivian and Samantha to check with
friends and teachers at school. Martin is still saddled
to the office fielding calls coming in from the public.

5. INT. NEW YORK PUBLIC SCHOOL—Vivian and Samantha
interview Gabe's teacher, THRESA BARKOWITZ, 40ish,
overwhelmed but committed. She says that Gabe was one of
her best students—a bit shy and reserved but bright and
attentive. *Until* about four or five months ago, when his
grades started to dip, his homework became erratic, he
rarely seemed to be paying attention . . . She's spoken
to the parents about it and they've been responsive, but
no one can figure out what the problem is and Gabe
doesn't let on that anything is the matter. Was it
drugs? Mrs. Barkowitz doesn't think so—kids grow up
fast these days and she certainly sees that, but no, it
didn't feel like that with him. It was more like, he
suddenly seemed mistrustful of everyone. The last time
she saw Gabe? The day he disappeared. She wanted to
throw a little party for him in class, for his
birthday . . .

6. FLASHBACK—Gabe comes alive in front of our eyes here in the classroom. Mrs. Barkowitz brings in a cake. The kids unenthusiastically sing "Happy Birthday." But when she presents him the cake, he refuses to blow out the candles. She gently prods him, and he dashes out of the room, wanting nothing to do with the celebration . . .

7. RESUME IN THE CLASSROOM—Mrs. Barkowitz says she found Gabe in the hall and asked him what was the matter, but all he could say was that "birthdays are stupid." And she couldn't get anything more out of him.

8. INT. FELDMAN APARTMENT—Dale tells Jack she noticed he was a little more moody lately, but nothing more than that. And she attributed it to the fact that they moved from the East Side about six months ago; she thought it might be that (he's not as close to his friends). But really, she thought this was just a phase he was going through—"You know how kids are, especially adolescents"—and she didn't want to make more out of it than it was or drag him from one child psychologist to the next and make him feel like a lab rat. "Of course," she admits, "he's my only child. It's not like I have much to compare it to." Jack asks why she didn't have more children. She figures that one is a handful, particularly with the hours that she and Bob work. She chastises herself for not paying more attention, for not taking Gabe's problems more seriously. And now . . . she can't believe he would have gone to the game and *sold* the ticket—what could he have been thinking? Or doing? What could he be involved in that she doesn't know about?

9. INT. GABE'S BEDROOM—Jack finds Danny and a COMPUTER
TECH working away on Gabe's computer. Turns out the kid
had been visiting porn sites on the Web. Danny thinks
it's pretty normal for an eleven year old. He remembers
what he was like at eleven. Jack says he barely knew
what girls looked like at that age, that Latin guys must
start younger. They get serious again as Jack asks if
there is any hint of child porn, a feasting area for
child predators. Danny says, "Not yet. But we're
looking." Jack asks what Gabe's screen name is. It's
gabeboard@globallink.com. Jack moves over to the
skateboard, takes it out, and looks at it (it's got a
"Thrasher" logo on it, just like the jacket). Jack
wonders aloud where eleven year olds skateboard around
here. Danny says there are some e-mails in here from his
friends about meeting down at Astor Place.

10. INT. FBI OFFICE—Martin interviews someone who's
come into the office, claiming to have seen Gabe. He
describes him in detail, an elaborate story about how he
saw him on the streets turning tricks. Martin asks the
"WITNESS" if he can remember what kind of jacket he was
wearing. The witness doesn't remember exactly. Martin
shows him a picture of a certain kind of jacket. The
witness says, "Yes, definitely, that was it." But he's
really shown him a picture of an entirely different
jacket. He sarcastically asks the witness if he enjoys
wasting their time. The witness stammers a
protestation, but Martin tells him to "get out of here."

11. EXT. ASTOR PLACE—Jack and Danny find an eclectic mix
of kids here—and pretty tough—not the group you'd

expect Gabe to be hanging out with. But sure enough, not
only does he hang out here, but he was here the night of
his disappearance. WALLY, one of his boarding friends,
tells them about that night . . . and Gabe appears . . .

**12. FLASHBACK—EXT. ASTOR PLACE—7:15 PM DOD—Yankee hat
now turned backward (to be cool). He has much more of a
street persona with them. He brags to his friends about
how he slipped his dad on the subway. Some say he's an
idiot for not going to a Yankee-Red Sox game, but Gabe
says, "Three hours of sitting alone having to listen
to my dad? Forget it!" He borrows a skateboard from one
of his buddies, does a pretty mean flip over the curb,
and . . .**

13. We RESUME in the PRESENT. What happened after that?
They hung around for a couple of hours, then went their
respective ways. Last time any of them saw him was
around nine, nine-thirty. Gabe was heading back uptown.

14. INT. FBI OFFICE—Martin fields calls of people who've
spotted Gabe around. He is polite, but aggravated at how
many of them there are. He sticks a pin in a map of the
city. There have been hundreds of "sightings." As he
hangs up, an AGENT tells him he's got another call. He
takes the phone, trying to be patient. Talks to the guy
on the other end. He saw Gabe walking around the Port
Authority. Asks him a question about the jacket
(picture in front of him). What color was the logo? He
gets it right. We read Martin's face: this one could be
real.

15. INT. PORT AUTHORITY—The entire team is here, spread out, looking for Gabe (based on the last tip). The NYPD is here, too. There are a lot of teenagers here. Some homeless kids, too. Suddenly Samantha spots Gabe across the way (walking with a GIRL), the Thrasher insignia right there on the back of his jacket. They rush over to him, calling his name, "Gabe, Gabe." But he doesn't turn. Finally, they catch up to him. Turn him around and . . . it's not him. It's another kid about eleven or twelve. But this kid is clearly a kid of the streets— tough, unkempt, probably unwashed. They make him take off the jacket. Check the label. Sure enough, it has Gabe's name tag emblazoned on it. Samantha looks at it, then, "Jack, it's got blood on it." As Jack looks at the bloodstains . . .

ACT THREE

1. INT. FBI INTERROGATION ROOM—The HOMELESS BOY insists for the tenth time that he never saw Gabe. He found the jacket on the floor by the lockers. What time? About 4 A.M. the night of Gabe's disappearance. Samantha interrupts Jack, pulls him out of the room: the girl who was with our homeless boy—her story corroborates his re: the jacket. And by the way, it turns out this kid has been missing for eight months. Parents live in Delaware. They're on their way. (Irony: They solved one case, just not the one they're on.)

2. INT. FBI COMMAND POST—The team assembled, trying to figure out their plan of attack. Vivian reports on the canvassing of the Port Authority. So far, no one remembers him, no evidence that he bought a ticket

anywhere, but the buses don't run past eleven, so he may have spent the night there and bought his ticket in the morning. They'll have to wait until the A.M. shift comes on to confirm. Recap using TIMELINE: they know he scalped his ticket at Yankee Stadium around 7 P.M., took a train to Astor Place, arrived around 8 P.M., hung out with his friends until 9–9:30, then the homeless kid found his jacket at the Port Authority at 4 A.M. Was he at the Port Authority? If so, why? Was he running away? Going to meet someone? And ran into trouble (the Port Authority is a tough place) while there? Kidnapped or killed: blood. Vivian notes that just because the jacket was found there doesn't mean the kid was ever there. Martin: "No, but maybe he was in the vicinity." He goes over to the map of the city—with the hundreds of pins of Gabe "sightings" from Staten Island to Harlem. Focuses on the area around the Port Authority. Three in the general vicinity. One report sights him at a cyber café at a time that fits the timeline. Jack tells Samantha to check it out (leaving Martin a bit stung). Danny's theory: It has something to do with those boarder kids. Maybe they turned on Gabe, ripped him off, beat him up, and that's how the blood got on the jacket. And a lot of those kids hang out at the Port Authority. He's going to revisit those kids. Vivian's going to the Port Authority to coordinate canvassing. An agent hands Jack a file. He reports to the gang: The blood on the jacket matches Gabe's blood type. Jack's got the unpleasant task of having to tell the parents and get something from the house with Gabe's DNA on it.

3. INT. FELDMAN HOUSE—EARLY MORNING—Parents look horrible, sleepless night, crying. Jack has to break

the news to them about the jacket and the blood. It's gut wrenching when he tells them he'll need Gabe's toothbrush for the DNA test.

4. INT. SCHOOLYARD—BROOKLYN—Danny finds SKATEBOARDING KIDS. Leans on them, tells them he knows they weren't being straight with him. If they care about Gabe, they have to tell him everything. They fess up: They were trying to protect their friends. When they left Astor Place that night, Gabe and the others were still there. But they heard the next day that the guys had gotten into some trouble, "messing with" some guy at one of the corner delis in the neighborhood. Danny: "Messing with how?" The kids downplay, nothing too rough, you know, sometimes they get their kicks shoplifting a candy bar or a soda. Just for fun.

5. INT. CYBER CAFÉ—Samantha confronts the sleazy Cyber OWNER. Got a call placing Gabe at the café the night of the disappearance. Owner denies—they don't allow anyone younger than sixteen. Samantha calls bullshit, knows this owner was busted before for letting in underagers (who'd gotten involved with child Internet porn). Under pressure, owner gives up the goods. Gabe did come in that night . . .

6. **FLASHBACK: Gabe appears in the café before their eyes, and we are BACK IN TIME: Distressed and trying to hold it together, Gabe asks owner if he can use one of the computers. The owner says he can't, he's not old enough, but Gabe begs him, just five minutes. He pulls out a few bucks. The owner says, "Five minutes." Gabe**

thanks him, heads for one of the computers, and fades away . . .

7. RESUME in the CYBER CAFÉ in the PRESENT. Owner swears he was only here for five minutes, and that was it. Owner says Gabe seemed distressed. Does he remember if the kid had blood on his jacket? No. He's told Samantha that. Which computer did he use? Owner doesn't remember exactly. One of the two in the corner.

8. INT. FBI OFFICE—Martin on the phone with Danny. He ran a check of criminal reports in the Astor Place area the night of the disappearance. Nothing came up, but he checked St. Vincent's Hospital. A KOREAN DELI OWNER checked himself into the ER with head wounds around 11 P.M.. Danny that's Martin ("good work")—trust may be forming between them.

9. INT. PORT AUTHORITY—Vivian with a ticket seller who recognizes Gabe's picture and remembers selling him a bus ticket sometime that night—late. But for the life of him, he can't remember where . . . Oh, wait a minute, yes he does. He remembers making a joke to the kid that he was going a long way, that he was going to visit the Alamo. Vivian: "So it was Texas?" Ticket seller: "Yes, definitely Texas." But they have twenty-five routes that go to Texas, and he has no idea which one it could be . . .

10. INT. KOREAN DELI—DELI OWNER (with bandage on his head) tells us what happened that night, and the deli comes alive . . .

11. FLASHBACK—SKATEBOARDERS (and Gabe) enter, just kind of screwing around. They swipe a couple of bags of chips and board out. Deli owner gives chase into the street. Everyone else is on a board, and they are too fast. But Gabe doesn't have his; he's on foot. Deli owner chases him into the alley and tackles him to the ground. A bit of a struggle. Gabe panics. Picks up a stray bottle, breaks it over deli owner's head . . .

12. RESUME IN DELI—Deli owner doesn't remember what happened after that. He was unconscious. Aroused a while later in the alley. Went to the hospital. He curses kids these days.

13. INT. FBI—Jack tells Martin: "Forensics just came in—the blood's not Gabe's. Must be the Korean deli owner's. Let's run a forensics comparison on his blood." Phone rings. It's Samantha.

14. INT. CYBER CAFÉ—Samantha with the computer techs. They managed to track Gabe's activity on the Web. Gabe had entered a chat room that night, and they've been able to decipher some of the words he wrote in the chat room: Is Jack ready for this? Here's what they could make out: "I'm in trouble . . ." then ready for this? "I'll come—Dad."

ACT FOUR

1. INT. FELDMAN HOUSE—Jack and Samantha confront Gabe's father, the mother by his side. The father insists he has no idea what they are talking about. That this is insane. Jack and Samantha remind them what they now

know: that Gabe got in trouble with the Korean deli owner, got to the Cyber Café, contacted someone he calls "Dad," went to the Port Authority, bought a bus ticket with the money he made from scalping the Yankee ticket, realized the jacket has blood on it, dumped it, and is now on his way to "Dad." Now, if they're hiding the kid because they are afraid he'll get in trouble, they should come clean now. Bob insists he has no idea what this is about. Why the hell would he communicate with his own son on-line? Jack: "Then who the hell is this 'Dad'?" Dale begins to crumble, realizing, "Oh my God. Oh my God." Bob realizes too, now, and admits the truth: Gabe is adopted. Jack and Samantha are dumbfounded: Why the hell didn't they tell them that before? The poor parents didn't think it was relevant—why should it matter? They adopted him when he was a baby, never thought of him as anything other than their own son. Samantha tells them that his adoptedness couldn't be more relevant: there are countless cases of real biological parents kidnapping children they'd given up years earlier. But Dale insists it doesn't make sense: Gabe never knew he was adopted. They never told him. Jack theorizes that Gabe did, in fact, find out. He had to—four or five months ago, when his behavior began to change. That would explain his rebelliousness, his moodiness, his reaction at school to the birthday party, his jilting his father at the Yankee game. He's somehow managed to find out who is real father is over the Internet. He's been communicating with him for months in a chat room, maybe thinking about someday seeing him. Then he stumbled into trouble with those kids and the deli owner, and he panicked. He didn't think he could turn to his own parents, so he reached

out to his biological father. And now he's on his way to
see him. Dale doesn't understand why. "Why would he turn
to a stranger instead of us?" Jack says: "Because he
doesn't trust you anymore. You lied to him. As far as
he's concerned, you've lied to him his whole life." The
parents are confounded with guilt and fear. And now Dale
realizes as she goes to a cubby in the hutch, when they
were moving six months ago, there was a box with his
adoption papers in it. She found it half open, but she
didn't think anything of it at the time. Gabe must have
gotten into it. Her heart is breaking for her son—oh my
God, for him to have found out that way. They should've
told him; she knew she should have told him a long time
ago. How could they have been so stupid? And he didn't
even feel like he could come to us? What have they done?
Then the father realizes the adoption papers don't give
the name of the biological parents, so how could he have
found out? Jack asks Dale to hand over the papers.

2. INT. ADOPTION AGENCY—Vivian talks to the ADOPTION
AGENT, manages to sweet-talk her way into finding out the
identity of the natural parents. Mother's name: Barbara
Young. Father: Mason Talber, but . . . he died three
years ago.

3. INT. FBI OFFICE—Gabe thinks he's on his way to meet
his father, whom he thinks he found on the Internet. But
his real father is dead. So whoever this "Dad" is, he's
major trouble. Danny has a hunch: he moves to the map of
Texas now posted on the wall. Unless he's on his way to
the northeastern-most town (the closest route to New
York), that bus wouldn't have arrived yet. If it's to
any of the other twenty-four routes, they can be sure he

didn't arrive yet. Let's try to track down the pedophile on-line, in the chat room Martin found. Jack says it's a chance worth taking.

4. INT. COMPUTER ROOM—Ten agents surfing chat rooms looking for "Dad." They find his screen name. Jack comes over. Tells TECHIE what to type. They're going to pretend to communicate with "Dad" as if they are Gabe. Jack tells techie to type, "It's Gabe. I had to get off the bus, and I am lost." Dad responds, "You forgot it?" Jack tells him to type, "I lost the piece of paper." But there is no response. Jack tells him to type: "Dad? Dad?" But he's gone . . . A techie reports that they tracked the origin of "Dad's" missives. It's from a Kinko's in San Antonio, Texas.

5. PLANE LANDING AT PRIVATE AIRPORT IN SAN ANTONIO

6. INT. KINKO'S—Jack talking to MANAGER at Kinko's. Running down a list of those who used the computers in the last few hours.

7. INT. FBI—Samantha calls Martin at Kinko's. She's gotten the rundown of convicted child molesters in the county. There are nine of them. But one of them, GRAYSON CHANDLER, works at Kinko's.

8. INT. GRAYSON CHANDLER'S HOUSE—Martin and Danny bust in, looking for him, but he's not there. They find pictures of Gabe, printed off a computer, on the kitchen counter.

9. EXT. GREYHOUND BUS STATION—SAN ANTONIO—Jack and
Vivian with local FBI stake out the area. Hoping that
Gabe is going to be on the bus. The bus pulls up. People
pile off, and then there's Gabe. Looking timid and
vulnerable, looking around, trying to figure out where
his "dad" is. Vivian wants to move in and grab Gabe. But
Jack says, "No. If we don't catch him taking possession
of the kid, then we've got nothing." A man emerges from
the periphery, coming toward Gabe. There he is. Jack,
Vivian creep in slowly. Grayson comes toward Gabe. Very
tense: How far do they have to let this go? Gabe
realizes it must be him. "Dad?" Grayson comes toward
him. Jack tells Vivian, "Not yet." Grayson goes to shake
his hand. Gabe takes it; their hands touch. Creepy. And
then Jack and Vivian move in, Vivian drawing her weapon,
Jack scooping up Gabe to safety. Gabe protesting, "What
are you doing? That's my dad. That's my dad."

10. INT. FBI OFFICE—Samantha waits with the Feldman
parents. They can't even begin to know what to say to
Gabe. None of this would have happened if they'd just
told him the truth about his adoption from the
beginning. Samantha says, "It's never too late to be
truthful. And believe me, he can take it." The rest of
the team enters with Gabe. Gabe doesn't move toward
them. He's still wary, mistrustful. Bob runs toward
him, wrapping him in his arms, crying. Hugging him like
he's never hugged him in his life. Dale joins them. They
hug and the family is reunited, but it's clear from
Gabe's face that they have some work to do to regain his
trust.

The following script is the actual shooting draft of "Birthday Boy." We wanted to demonstrate how a story evolves from a drama outline written in prose to a script written in dialogue. Please keep in mind that each show has its own style and format. We are showing you this one from *Without a Trace* strictly as an example.

Executive Producer: Jerry Bruckheimer
Executive Producer: Jonathan Littman
Executive Producer: Ed Redlich
Co-Executive Producer: Hank Steinberg
Co-Executive Producer: Jacob Epstein
Producer: Steve Beers
Producer: Jan Nash
Producer: Greg Walker

WITHOUT A TRACE

"Birthday Boy"

Episode One - GL#175651

Written by
Hank Steinberg

Directed by
David Nutter

Production Draft - White - July 16, 2002
Blue Revisions (Full Script) - July 19, 2002
Pink Revisions (Full Script) - July 19, 2002
Yellow Revisions (Pages 16-19) - July 29, 2002
Green Revisions (Pages 20,50,54,56) - July 29, 2002
Goldenrod Revisions (Pages 40-41) - July 30, 2002
Salmon Revisions (Pages 11-11B) - September 9, 2002

WITHOUT A TRACE

"Birthday Boy"

<u>TEASER</u>

1   EXT. MANHATTAN - 6 P.M. - AN EARLY FALL DAY   1

Sweeping OVERHEAD SHOTS of the glorious city. Teeming with
people. Cabs and buses. People headed hither and yon at the
end of a long week. We make our way DOWN to a SUBWAY STATION
at 57th Street...

1A   INT. 57TH STREET SUBWAY STATION - CONTINUOUS   1A

Amongst the crowd, we FIND 40ish BOB FREEDMAN descending the
STAIRCASE with his eleven year old son GABE. Father (wearing
NY Cap) and son (dressed a bit more hip, wearing a
distinctive "Thrash Dog" jacket, and NY cap) obviously headed
for the ball game.

                BOB
      ...and we used to sit there in the
      bleachers, in that short right
      field, and we could practically
      touch Roger Maris.

                GABE
    Yeah? How about Mickey Mantle?

                BOB
      He was all the way in center, which
      was four hundred sixty-five feet
      back then.

He hands Gabe his ticket.

                BOB (cont'd)
      Happy Birthday, kiddo.

                GABE
    Thanks.

Bob messes with Gabe's hat. Gabe moves away, slightly
annoyed, maybe at that age where he doesn't like being
touched.

                BOB
    You go first.

Bob swipes the card. Gabe goes through the turnstile. Bob
swipes it again, the turnstile locks. He swipes it again,
again it locks, realizes the card is tapped. Damn.

                (CONTINUED)

1A   CONTINUED: 1A

                              BOB (cont'd)
                    Stay right there. I gotta add more
                    money to this.

Bob retreats to the TICKET BOOTH to renew his Metro card.
But there's a couple of people ahead of him on line.

The train pulls into the station. Gabe heads for it. Bob
looks back.

                              BOB (cont'd)
                    Wai--

But he realizes Gabe can't hear him. He gets to the front of
the line, hands the Teller ten dollars, turns, sees Gabe
heading for the train as the doors open. Gabe waves to him,
"Hurry up!"

Teller hands Bob back his card. He hurries for the
turnstile, swipes the card, moves through, gets caught.
Looks back, his sweater. Shit. Untangles it.

Gabe's in the subway, standing by the open door. He gets
pushed deeper into the car as three big guys pile in. Bob
hurries, but the doors close.

                              BOB (cont'd)
                    Hey! Open the doors! Open the
                    doors!

But the subway starts to move. Gabe screams into the window.

                              BOB (cont'd)
                    Get off at the next stop!

He runs alongside the subway now, screaming, the roar of the
moving train drowning out his voice, his son disappearing
into the dark tunnel, into oblivion...

2   EXT. YANKEE STADIUM - 9AM THE FOLLOWING - DAY   2

The D train, now high above-ground, rumbles into the 161st
Street Station at the Stadium. We BOOM DOWN to the Stadium,
where a handful of Yankee employees prepare for the day game
which begins in a few hours...

We SWEEP PAST NEWS CREWS, overhearing one REPORTER talking
into her CAMERA:

                                                        (CONTINUED)

2   CONTINUED: 2

                              REPORTER
                  ...what began as a classic American
                  rite of passage -- a father taking
                  his son to a baseball game on his
                  eleventh birthday -- has become the
                  worst American nightmare...

We CONTINUE PAST to FIND "Missing" Posters with Gabe's
picture posted all over the place. NYPD everywhere as Yankee
employees begin to arrive for work.

ANGLE ON JACK and SAMANTHA at the scene:

                              JACK
                  The father says he thought Gabe
                  would get off at the next stop, so
                  he got on the next train to follow
                  him. When he wasn't there, he took
                  the train all the way up here.
                  Checked the platform, checked the
                  gate, finally tried the seats.

                              SAMANTHA
                  The boy had his own ticket?

                              JACK
                  Apparently.

                              SAMANTHA
                  And then the father called NYPD?

                              JACK
                  Yeah. About seven last night.

                              SAMANTHA
                      (annoyed)
                  And they waited 'til this morning
                  to call us?

                              JACK
                  I know.

VIVIAN approaches:

                              VIVIAN
                  The Yankees are bringing in
                  everyone who worked last night.
                  Hopefully someone saw something.

                                                          (CONTINUED)

2   CONTINUED: (2)   2

                              SAMANTHA
                    We don't even know if the kid ever
                    made it here.

                              JACK
                    Even if he did, it was perfect
                    weather last night. And the Red
                    Sox. There were fifty thousand
                    people. Probably ten thousand kids
                    his age.

2A   **EXT. YANKEE STADIUM - CONTINUOUS**   2A

       **JACK'S POV: Gabe appears, a few yards away, tantalizingly
       close for a moment, but then a crowd fills in around him and
       Gabe disappears from sight within it...**

2B   EXT. YANKEE STADIUM - 9AM DAY - RESUMING   2B

                              JACK
                    Why would anybody have noticed him?

       The CROWD fades away, leaving only Gabe, but then he fades
       away, too -- gone.

3   INT. FBI - COMMAND POST - 10:15 AM   3   *

       On the TIMELINE, one mere fact: "6:05 PM - Got on Uptown D-
       Train at 57th Street."

       Gabe's picture up on the BOARD. His name next to it, "GABE   *
       FREEDMAN". We PUSH into it and into CREDITS...   *

                              END TEASER

Without A Trace Episode #1 "Birthday Boy" (Pink) 7/19/02   5.

ACT ONE

4   INT. FBI - COMMAND POST - 10:15 AM (16 HOURS MISSING)   4

Jack debriefs Samantha, Vivian, DANNY and MARTIN.

> JACK
> He got on that subway at 6:05 and
> unfortunately that's all we've got
> so far. Missing sixteen hours and
> counting.

> DANNY
> How do we even know that? The
> father's word?

> SAMANTHA
> We ran his Metrocard, it supports
> his story.

> MARTIN
> But there are no eyewitnesses?

> SAMANTHA
> Tons of eyewitnesses. Just none
> that we can find.

> DANNY
> Who's covering the Stadium?

> JACK
> Are you kidding? That's Viv.

> VIVIAN
> Not exactly the way I wanted to
> meet Derek Jeter.

> DANNY
> (ribbing her)
> You know, this never would have
> happened at Shea.

> VIVIAN
> It's sad, how bitter Met fans are.

> JACK
> Danny, you pick up subway detail
> with the NYPD.

He gestures to a big subway map on the wall:

> JACK (cont'd)
> Focus on this area here, and up
> through the Bronx.

(CONTINUED)

4   CONTINUED:
                                                                        4

                              SAMANTHA
                      (indicating a stack of
                       files on the table)
                   I'm into convicted child-abusers
                   and pedophiles in the same
                   vicinity.

                              JACK
                   Start with the ones above 57th
                   Street. If he was lifted at that
                   time of day, it was probably by
                   someone on his way home. Now then,
                   Mr. Fitzgerald...

They all look at Martin.

                              JACK (cont'd)
                   We've got a missing kid all over
                   the news so we're gonna get a lot
                   of incoming calls on this one.
                   Most'll be bogus but they all have
                   to be run down.

                              MARTIN
                      (disappointed)
                   So you want me here.

                              JACK
                   You break a major protocol on your
                   first day, that's what happens.
                      (exiting)
                   All right, let's go.

They move out. Martin comes over to Samantha and Danny,
wanting to reach out to his comrades.

                              MARTIN
                   How long does it take to get out of
                   his doghouse?

                              DANNY
                   Depends on the dog.

Danny slaps Martin's shoulder with mock affection and heads
out. Samantha half-shrugs, smiles at Martin.

                              SAMANTHA
                   Don't mind Danny. He's just marking   *
                   his territory.   *

And she heads out.

                                                    (CONTINUED)

4   CONTINUED: (2)   4

ANGLE ON Jack and Vivian:

                    VIVIAN
          You gonna polygraph the father?

                         JACK
          We'll see.
               (almost to himself)
          I hate this part.

5   INT. FREEDMAN APARTMENT - DINING ROOM - 11 AM (17 HOURS   5
      MISSING)

We PAN ACROSS pictures on the LIVING ROOM wall. Dale in a
nurse's uniform with co-workers at a hospital. Family
pictures with Gabe. From new-born baby to the present day...

We FIND Bob emotionally telling his story to Jack. His wife
DALE sitting by his side (bassinet, diapers, evidence of a
new-born around).

                    BOB
          I thought he understood what I was
          saying. But then he wasn't at 66th
          Street so I assumed he must have
          gone ahead to the Stadium.

He glances at Dale with horrible guilt, then back to Jack:

                    BOB (cont'd)
          God I don't know what I was
          thinking.

He gets up, extremely agitated, hating himself:

                    BOB (cont'd)
          I don't know why I didn't call the
          police right away.

Jack looks at Bob, then at Dale.

                    JACK
          I know this is difficult, but would
          you mind if I spoke to your husband
          alone?

                    DALE
          Oh...of course. It's about time to
          feed the baby anyway.

She heads out, pauses to look at Bob, wanting to connect,
trying to hold it together herself.

                                        (CONTINUED)

Without A Trace Episode #1 "Birthday Boy" (Pink) 7/19/02   7A.

5   CONTINUED: 5

But Bob is too busy chastising himself to notice. She exits.
Bob looks at Jack, "okay, let's go."

5A   INT.   FREEDMAN LIVING ROOM - A FEW MINUTES LATER   5A

Jack and Bob reconvened for private interview. Jack taking
notes. Bob's clearly uncomfortable with the tenor of the
questioning.

                         JACK
               Are you having any financial
               problems?

                         BOB
                    (what's this about?)
               We struggle like everybody.

                         JACK
               Any problems in your marriage?

                                                    (CONTINUED)

Without A Trace Episode #1 "Birthday Boy" (Pink) 7/19/02   8.

5A   CONTINUED: 5A

> BOB
> Beyond the normal marital stuff,
> no.

> JACK
> What do you mean, normal marital
> stuff?

> BOB
> I don't understand how this is
> remotely relevant to anything.

> JACK
> It may not be, but I have to ask.

> BOB
> Some sick son of a bitch may be out
> there with my son and you're in
> here asking me questions about my
> marriage.

Jack puts down his pen, pushes his pad aside.

> JACK
> Look, I've worked hundreds of these
> cases, okay? And there are certain
> patterns that develop. Patterns
> that I don't like but just because
> I don't like them doesn't mean I
> can ignore them. Do you want to
> know what they are?

Bob gestures: go ahead.

> JACK (cont'd)
> When a child disappears, the person
> who claims they saw them last is
> very often the one who took them.
> And when that person is a parent,
> the incidence doubles. Now my gut
> tells me you're okay, but I can't   *
> know that for sure until you let me   *
> in. That's the only way you can   *
> earn my trust and that's the only   *
> way I'm going to be able to include   *
> you in what we do.   *

> BOB
> Next thing you'll be asking me to
> take a lie-detector.

(CONTINUED)

5A   CONTINUED: (2)   5A

                              JACK
                    That's usually the case, but right   *
                    now I'm not asking you for that.   *

6   INT.   57TH STREET SUBWAY STATION - 12 PM (18 HOURS MISSING) 6

MISSING FLYERS with Gabe's picture hang all over here now.
NYPD shows flyers to Beggars and Musicians who haunt this
STATION, trying to find a witness.

FIND Danny on the PLATFORM talking to NYPD guys, who are
coming up with nothing. Disappointment reading on their
faces.

7   OMITTED   7

8   EXT.   YANKEE STADIUM - 12:30 PM (18.5 HOURS MISSING)   8

Vivian talking to NYPD and a Head Usher, who shakes his head,
no one's seen Gabe.

9   INT.   FREEDMAN APARTMENT - 2 PM (20 HOURS MISSING)   9

Jack and Bob, who's getting to the end of his rope:

                    JACK
          Did you usually give Gabe his own
          ticket to hold?

               BOB
          No.

                    JACK
          Then why yesterday?

               BOB
          It was his birthday. He's eleven.

Jack looks at him: what's that mean?

                    BOB (CONT'D)
               (irritated)
          I wanted him to feel like he was
          old enough to be trusted with it.

                    JACK
          Okay. Have you and Gabe been   *
          fighting about anything lately?   *

               BOB
          No.

                    JACK
          Did he ever play hookie from
          school?

                                          (CONTINUED)

Drama Outline and Script | 141

9   CONTINUED: 9

                          BOB
               No.

                          JACK
               Does he have any friends that might
               get him into trouble?

                          BOB
               No.

                          JACK
               Is he involved with drugs?

     Bob looks at him a long time, shakes his head.

                          BOB
               No.

10   INT. FBI OFFICE - COMMAND POST - 3PM (21 HOURS MISSING)   10

     Martin on the phone.

(CONTINUED)

10   CONTINUED: 10

                         MARTIN
              You think you saw him where?...
              Okay...And this was what time?...

Martin grabs a push-pin, sticks it into a huge map of the
city.

                         MARTIN (cont'd)
              Thank you. No, we appreciate it.
              Every tip is useful.

But as Martin goes to jot down the information, we WIDEN on
the MAP to see that there are hundreds of pins -- marking the
hundreds of supposed "Gabe sightings."

11   OMITTED   11

12   OMITTED   12

13   EXT. 154TH STREET SUBWAY STATION - 4 PM (22 HOURS MISSING)13

Danny shows a picture of Gabe to a wheel-chaired VIOLINIST
(violin case open with coins and dollars in it):

                         VIOLINIST
              Yeah, I seen him.

                         DANNY
              You're sure?

                         VIOLINIST
                  (with attitude)
              Yeah I'm sure. He come up to me
              yesterday, must've been about six,   *
              six-thirty...   *

And now Gabe appears in the SCENE and we are BACK IN TIME...

13A   **EXT. 154TH STREET SUBWAY STATION - 6:30 PM DOD**   13A

**Gabe comes down the steps, looking around, realizing he's
probably not in the right place. Sees a Violinist in a
wheelchair, playing for money.**

                         GABE
              **Excuse me...this isn't the stop for
              Yankee Stadium, is it?**

                         VIOLINIST
              **You got off too soon. It's the next
              one. 161st Street.**

                                                  (CONTINUED)

13A   CONTINUED: 13A

                              GABE
                    Thanks.

**He takes a crumpled dollar out of his pocket and drops it in
the Violinist's box.**

                            VIOLINIST
                    I like your jacket.

Gabe smiles, flattered.

                              GABE
                    Thanks.

Violinist looks slightly away from Gabe...

13B   EXT. 154TH STREET SUBWAY STATION - 4 PM   13B
        (22 HOURS MISSING) - RESUMING

                            VIOLINIST
                    He went back up to the subway and
                    that was it.

Gabe fades away and we realize the Violinist is now talking
to Danny. We are back in the PRESENT...

                              DANNY
                    Did he mention his father?

                            VIOLINIST
                    Nope.

                              DANNY
                    And he didn't seem nervous or
                    worried?

                            VIOLINIST
                    No. He just seemed like a nice kid
                    on his way to the ball game.

14   STYLISTIC TIME-LINE SHOT: 14

        6:30 PM - Gets off Subway at 154th Street

        6:35 PM - Gets on Next Subway to Yankee Stadium (?)

14AA   INT. FBI OFFICES - COMMAND POST - DAY   14AA   *

        Martin's map of "Gabe Sightings" with even more red push-pins   *
        than before. Samantha approaches, eyes the board.   *

                            SAMANTHA   *
                    Lot of little red dots.   *

                                                      (CONTINUED)

Without A Trace Episode #1 "Birthday Boy" (Salmon) 9/9/02   11A.

14AA   CONTINUED: 14AA

>   MARTIN
>   Phone's ringing every fifteen
>   seconds. Must be a lot of little
>   brown-haired kids unaccounted for.
>   (then)
>   One woman keeps calling, telling me
>   she's convinced she saw Gabe on TV
>   this morning ringing the bell to
>   open the stock exchange.

>   SAMANTHA
>   Trouble is, just when it seems like
>   every nut in America has your phone
>   number, that's the exact moment a
>   live one comes in.

>   MARTIN
>   Better come in soon, I'm running
>   out of push-pins.

Martin puts in the last of the push-pins. Under which an ND
Agent hands Samantha a slip of paper.

>   SAMANTHA
>   (off slip)
>   I've got a guy, Gerald Dearborn,
>   recently paroled for lewd acts with
>   a minor -- a neighbor saw him on
>   118th Street having breakfast at a
>   McDonald's with a little dark-
>   haired kid... What have you got up
>   around Morningside Heights?

>   MARTIN
>   Two sightings. One around 125th
>   Street, the other outside the
>   Columbia gym, both around nine
>   o'clock.

>   SAMANTHA
>   See? Could be our live one.

She's about to head off.

>   MARTIN
>   Need an extra body?

Martin's phone ringing, under...

>   SAMANTHA
>   (sympathetic)
>   Next time.

Without A Trace Episode #1 "Birthday Boy" (Salmon) 9/9/02   11B.

14A   INT.   HARLEM TENEMENT - STAIRWELL - SIMULTANEOUS   14A

Two NYPD and a plainclothes PAROLE OFFICER. Samantha (in FBI
jacket) and two other FBI Agents enter.

                    PAROLE OFFICER
          The neighbor saw Dearborn this
          morning with a boy sounds like he
          could be yours.

                    SAMANTHA
          Let's go.

Without A Trace Episode #1 "Birthday Boy" (Pink) 7/19/02   12.

14B   OMITTED   14B   *

14C   INT. DEARBORN'S APARTMENT - MOMENTS LATER   14C   *

A POLICE RAM bursts through the door. In come the cops and
Samantha, guns out to FIND...

DEARBORN sitting on his couch, listening to music with noise-   *
filter headphones. He turns to them --

                    DEARBORN   *
              What are you doing?   *

Samantha moves deeper into the apartment, no sign of Gabe.   *
Finds stacks of videos. Picks one up. Then finds a teen boy   *
magazine. On her distasteful expression...   *

15   OMITTED   15

16   INT. FREEDMAN APARTMENT - GABE'S ROOM - 6 PM (24 HOURS   16
      MISSING)

Jack walks around the room, taking it all in, gazing at
Gabe's posters, his clothes, his possessions, his desk, a
skateboard in the corner.

Without A Trace Episode #1 "Birthday Boy" (Pink) 7/19/02   13.

16A   **INT.   FREEDMAN APARTMENT - GABE'S ROOM - EVENING**   16A

JACK'S POV: GABE'S GHOST APPEARS, SITTING AT HIS COMPUTER, TYPING AWAY ON THE INTERNET.

16B   INT. FREEDMAN APARTMENT - GABE'S ROOM - 6 PM (24 HOURS   16B
      MISSING) - RESUMING

Dale enters, cradling her year-old baby in her arms. As Jack
looks over at her, **Gabe fades away.**

                    DALE
          You wanted to speak to me alone?

                    JACK
            (re: baby)
          When you're ready.

                    DALE
          That's all right. She's asleep.

                    JACK
          She's beautiful.

                    DALE
          Gabe could never get to sleep when
          he was this age. He had so much
          energy.
            (off Jack's smile)
          I want to apologize for Bob. He
          knows you're just doing your job.

                    JACK
          If I were in his shoes, I'd be a
          lot less patient than he was.

                    DALE
          Do you have children?

                    JACK
          Two girls.

                    DALE
          How old?

                    JACK
          Six and eight.

                    DALE
          That must be nice. To have them so
          close in age.

                                        (CONTINUED)

.6B   CONTINUED: 16B

                    JACK
          Yeah, it is.

                    DALE
          I've heard that...

She doesn't know how to say this but has to.

16B   CONTINUED: (2)   16B

> DALE (cont'd)
> ...if you don't find a child in the
> first 48 hours that he's
> probably...

She can't say the rest. Jack looks at her sympathetically.

> JACK
> It's a good thing we're involved as
> soon as we are. That's not always
> the case.

A beat. That's not really a satisfying answer and they both
know it. His cell phone rings.

> JACK (cont'd)
> Yeah.

Dale watches his expression change, realizing there's news.

> JACK (cont'd)
> Well get back to the office and run
> the prints...Right. Bye.

He hangs up, looks at expectant Dale:

> JACK (cont'd)
> Somebody showed up in Gabe's seat
> yesterday in the third inning,
> after your husband had already come
> and gone. Luckily, he struck up a
> conversation with the people in the
> seats next to him. He claims he
> bought the ticket from a scalper
> outside the Stadium.

> DALE
> (scared)
> How would a scalper have gotten
> Gabe's ticket?

> JACK
> I don't know but we'll find out.

17   INT. FBI OFFICE - 6:30 PM (24.5 HOURS MISSING)   17

Vivian at her CUBICLE, finger-print images race across her
computer screen. Martin comes over.

> MARTIN
> What've you got?

(CONTINUED)

17   CONTINUED: 17

                         VIVIAN
              The stub from Gabe's ticket. There
              were six partial prints on it, I'm
              trying to find a match....How's the
              office treating you?

                         MARTIN
              The office is fine. I think Danny's   *
              got a bit of a problem with me.   *

                         VIVIAN
              Well, when you caught that he   *
              missed something on that alibi last   *
              week, you didn't need to bring it   *
              up in front of everyone. Unless you   *
              were trying to show him up. Or show   *
              off.   *

Martin is taken aback by her frankness but considers that she *
may be right...   *

                         VIVIAN (CONT'D)
              Here we go.

INSERT COMPUTER SCREEN: The prints match.

She hits a button.

INSERT COMPUTER SCREEN: The face of a FELON comes up. Name:
GEORGE LINCOLN.

                         VIVIAN (cont'd)
              George Lincoln. Auto theft, petty
              larceny, did ten months at Rikers.   *

                         MARTIN
                   (this is the guy)
              And he lives in the Bronx.

Vivian scoops up the phone to make an urgent call...

18   EXT. STREET - BRONX - 10 PM (28 HOURS MISSING)   18

Jack and Samantha wait in their CAR. On a stakeout. Jack   *
listening to something in an earpiece, then speaks into a
remote mike.

                         JACK
              Okay then, cover the back.
                   (looks at Samantha)
              His apartment's clean.

A beat as they prepare for what could be a long wait.

                                           (CONTINUED)

18   CONTINUED: 18

                        SAMANTHA
          How are the parents holding up?

                        JACK
          Not great.

                        SAMANTHA
          Did you polygraph the father?

                                                        (CONTINUED)

18   CONTINUED: (2)   18

                         JACK
              No. Not yet. Let's see what we get
              from Mr. Lincoln.   *

Danny and Vivian in another CAR across the street.   *

                         DANNY
              Say what you want about the middle
              of our lineup, but the guys who
              scalp at Shea are good family men.

                         VIVIAN
              Do you realize if it weren't for
              poor Bill Buckner, it'd be thirty
              years since the Mets won the World
              Series. That's before you were even
              born, isn't it?

                         DANNY
              Wait, here he is.

ANGLE ON LINCOLN crossing the street toward his apartment,
headed toward the sidewalk about halfway between Danny and
Vivian's position and Jack and Samantha's.

Danny and Vivian get out of their car and move discreetly   *
toward him. Jack and Samantha do the same from the other
direction.

Lincoln senses the approach, slows his step, spies both teams
converging, veers away.

Danny grabs his gun but doesn't point it.

                         DANNY (CONT'D)
              George Lincoln, FBI. We need to
              talk to you.

Lincoln stops in his tracks.

19   INT. FBI OFFICE - 10:30 PM (28.5 HOURS MISSING)   19   *

Jack shows a picture of Gabe to Lincoln.   *

                         JACK   *
              You recognize him?   *
                                                                    *
                                                                    *

                                                      (CONTINUED)

Drama Outline and Script | 153

19   CONTINUED: 19

                              LINCOLN   *
                    I bought a ticket off him   *
                    yesterday. So what?   *

                              JACK   *
                    he's missing and you're the last   *
                    person who saw him, that's what.   *

                              LINCOLN
                    Aw man, I don't know nothin' about   *
                    that. All I did was a little
                    business with the kid...

WE PUSH IN ON Lincoln and make our way BACK IN TIME...

20   **EXT.   STREET CORNER NEAR YANKEE STADIUM - 7 PM DOD**   20

**Beneath the subway tracks, Lincoln wheels and deals. Gabe
approaches, waits for a moment as Lincoln completes another
deal. Then Gabe comes over.**

                              GABE
                    I got one.

                              LINCOLN
                         (reaching for ticket)
                    All right, little man, lemme see.

                              GABE
                    I hold it. You look.

Lincoln laughs.

                              LINCOLN
                    You's a smart little cracker, ain't ya?

Gabe shows him the ticket.

                              LINCOLN (CONT'D)
                    I give you thirty bucks for it.

                              GABE
                    Face value's forty-five.

                              LINCOLN
                    It's a single, man. And game's
                    about to start.

                              GABE
                    It's the Red Sox and it's a sell-out.

                                                      (CONTINUED)

20   CONTINUED: 20

> LINCOLN
> All right, I'll give you face.

>   GABE
> Fifty.

Lincoln laughs again.

>   GABE (cont'd)
> Fifty or I'm walking.

On Lincoln grinning, enjoying this savvy kid...

21   INT. FBI OFFICE - RESUMING   21   *

>   LINCOLN
> I gave him fifty. He went his way,
> I went mine.

>   VIVIAN
> You see <u>where</u> he went?

>   LINCOLN
> Nah man, on to the next, you know.   *

Jack and Vivian share a look.   *

>   LINCOLN (CONT'D)   *
> Look, I got fifteen other guys   *
> who'll put me at the Stadium 'til   *
> eleven o'clock.   *

>   JACK   *
>   (to ND Agent)   *
> Get the names.   *

Jack gets up. Vivian follows.   *

22   INT. FBI COMMAND POST - CONTINUOUS   22   *

Jack and Vivian entering, passing Danny.   *

>   JACK   *
> Lincoln's clean.   *

                                                    (CONTINUED)

22   CONTINUED: 22

                            VIVIAN   *
                 Savvy little kid, huh?

                            DANNY   *
                          (to Vivian)
                 He knew enough to blow off the
                 Yankees.

                            JACK
                 Yeah, and his father.

Jack moves to the TIMELINE, which now shows:

7 PM - Sells Ticket to SCALPER

                            JACK (cont'd)
                 Where the hell was he going?

BOOM UP to the picture of Gabe on the BOARD. Who is this
kid?

                        END ACT ONE   *

ACT TWO

23   INT. FBI COMMAND POST - 7 AM NEXT DAY (37 HOURS MISSING) 23

Jack and the team: debriefing.

> JACK
> All right, it's been thirty-seven hours
> and he's slipping away from us.
> (throwing to Samantha at
> the timeline)
> Sam.
>   *

> SAMANTHA
> We know Gabe got to Yankee Stadium
> and sold his ticket for fifty
> bucks. That was at seven o'clock
> Friday night. The question is:
> where was he going after that?

> MARTIN
> His parents have no idea?

> JACK
> If they did, they would've
> volunteered it already. And I want
> to find out more before I go back
> to them.

> DANNY
> Maybe it's not like his father
> says. Maybe the kid gave him the
> slip on the subway.

> SAMANTHA
> He didn't <u>know</u> his father's
> Metrocard would be tapped.

> DANNY
> No, but he didn't have to get on
> the train, did he? He could've
> waited to make sure his father made
> it through the turnstile.

> VIVIAN
> Well, he obviously didn't want to
> go to the game. Though I can't
> figure that.

> DANNY
> He's eleven. He thinks going to the
> ball game with his Dad is lame.
> He's got friends or a girlfriend or
> something better to do.
> (MORE)

(CONTINUED)

23   CONTINUED: 23

> DANNY (cont'd)
> Maybe he was gonna wait 'til they
> got to the game, tell his dad he's
> going to the bathroom and take off.
> Then he gets this lucky break with
> the subway and he takes it. And now
> he's got an extra fifty bucks in
> his pocket to show off with his
> friends.

> JACK
> Well if you're right, that's one
> pissed-off kid.

> VIVIAN
> Yeah, but he's not so pissed off to
> not come home for 37 hours. He's
> never done anything like this
> before, he's never even played
> hookie...

> SAMANTHA
> According to his parents.

> JACK
> Viv's right. Something happened to
> him between seven o'clock and
> whenever he was planning on showing
> up that night at home.

> MARTIN
> You don't think there's any chance
> he just ran away?

> JACK
> Of course there's a chance. But why
> that day? Why like that?

A beat. Nobody has an answer. Danny tries...

> DANNY
> He took his fifty bucks, got back
> on the subway and went to meet
> somebody.

> SAMANTHA
> Which means we've got to profile
> this kid like he's an adult. Find
> out everything about him.

> JACK
> Exactly. Let's get on it.

24   INT.   PUBLIC SCHOOL - CLASSROOM - 8 AM (38 HOURS MISSING)   24

Blackboard.   Child art projects on the wall.   Little desks.
32 year old spunky, Hispanic, MARIA FLORES, sits on the edge
of the window sill, clearly shaken by Gabe's disappearance.

                    FLORES
          I know I'm not supposed to play
          favorites, but this is my second year
          with him and Gabe's one of those kids
          that when I go home at the end of the
          day I feel like, no matter how tired I
          am, it's worth it.

                    VIVIAN
          Well you're here on a Sunday
          morning. That says a lot.

                    FLORES
          Yeah, like, I'm way too slow at
          grading papers.

                    SAMANTHA
          How's Gabe in class?

She shakes her head to herself, as if she's got something she
can't quite face.

                    SAMANTHA (CONT'D)
          What is it?

                    FLORES
          I could just shoot myself.
              (off their looks)
          I didn't think anything about it at
          the time but now this...he was
          usually so attentive, such a good
          student, but lately, I don't know,
          I think something might have been
          different with him.

                    VIVIAN
          Like what?

                    FLORES
          I don't know. It was very subtle.
          Hard to describe but something was
          different.

                    SAMANTHA
          Drugs?

                                        (CONTINUED)

24   CONTINUED: 24

                              FLORES
                I don't know. I didn't think so,
                but now I don't know. Maybe I'm
                crazy because of what's
                happened...but then, his birthday,
                the last time I saw him, we made a
                cake and we all sang "Happy
                Birthday" and he just ran out of
                the room. I tried to talk to him
                about it after school, but he just
                sat there...

24A   INT. PUBLIC SCHOOL - CLASSROOM - DAY   24A

And Gabe appears, sitting sullenly at his desk.

                              FLORES
                What's the matter, Gabe? Talk to
                me.

                              GABE
                I told you nothing.

                              FLORES
                Nothing's the matter but you react
                like that to Happy Birthday.

                              GABE
                Birthday's are stupid.

Flores comes over to him, pulls up a chair, close.

                              FLORES
                Is something going on at home?

                              GABE
                Everything's fine. Can I go,
                please?

                              FLORES
                Okay, but whatever it is, I want
                you to know I'm here. Okay?

24B   INT. PUBLIC SCHOOL - CLASSROOM - 8 AM (38 HOURS MISSING) 24B
        RESUMING

Flores turns back to Vivian and Samantha and **Gabe fades
away...**

                              FLORES
                I was going to talk to his parents
                about it on Monday, but now I guess
                it's too late.

25   INT.   FREEDMAN APARTMENT - DEN - 9 AM (39 HOURS MISSING)   25

Dale -- trying to hold it together emotionally but the
strength we saw from her in the Teaser is receding. Jack
sits across from her, looking at her empathetically.

                    DALE
          I can't imagine what that was
          about. He seemed fine this   *
          morning. And I thought he was   *
          excited about going to the game   *
          with his dad.   *

                    JACK
          His teacher says he's been
          withdrawn lately. Did you notice
          that?

                    DALE
          She said that?
              (off his nod)
          God, maybe a little, but I thought
          it was probably just his reaction
          to the baby. Or to moving.

                    JACK
          You never mentioned that you moved.

Dale -- trying to put the pieces together herself...

                    DALE
          Yeah, about six months ago. How
          could he have gone to that game and
          sold that ticket -- what is he
          involved in that I don't know
          about?

26   INT.   FREEDMAN APARTMENT - HALLWAY - MOMENTS LATER   26

Jack walks down the hall as Bob emerges from the BEDROOM in a
robe, unshaven, looking like shit. A long beat as they size
each other up.

                                                    (CONTINUED)

26   CONTINUED: 26

>   BOB
>   You were right. Asking me those
>   questions. Apparently there was
>   some stuff going on with Gabe we
>   didn't know about.

>   JACK
>   Every parent can say that.

Bob peers into the other room, eyeing Dale.

>   BOB
>   I know she thinks it's my fault.   *
>   She won't say it, but I see it in
>   her eyes.

>   JACK
>   I don't think so.

A long beat.

>   BOB
>   I'd like to take that polygraph. If
>   that's all right?

>   JACK
>   We'll set it up.

He continues past Jack down the hall. Jack makes his way
into...

27   INT.   FREEDMAN APARTMENT - GABE'S ROOM - CONTINUOUS   .27

...where he finds Danny and a Computer Tech working away on
Gabe's computer.

>   JACK
>   Got anything?

>   DANNY
>   He was surfing a few of the porn
>   sites.

Jack leans over, has a look at the laptop screen, shakes his
head at the graphic nature of the image.

>   JACK
>   I barely knew what girls looked
>   like when I was that age.

>   DANNY
>   I was all over it. Since I was
>   eight.

                                            (CONTINUED)

27   CONTINUED: 27

Jack lets that one go. He peers into the hall, closes the
door.

                    JACK
          Any weird chat rooms?

                    DANNY
          No. This kid doesn't feel like
          predator prey to me.

Jack moves over to the skateboard, picks it up, it's got a
bunch of stickers on it. He sees a "Thrash Dog" sticker, the
same logo that's on the jacket Gabe was wearing. Turns it
over, looks at the wheels: they're worn.

                    JACK
          I wonder where an eleven year old
          would skateboard around here.

                    DANNY
          There's some emails here from his
          friends, talk about some old
          loading ramps, on the west side, by
          the river.

Jack looks at the skateboard.

28   INT.   FBI OFFICE - 10 AM (40 HOURS MISSING)   28

A TV in the corner shows a News Anchor reporting on the news
of the "Missing Birthday Boy" with Gabe's picture. PAN from
this TV to Martin at his CUBICLE, interviewing a haggard
50ish, bearded man (WITNESS).

                    WITNESS
          So I'm there feeding the pigeons,
          'cause you know it's nice right
          there by the water and I see this
          kid, can't be more than twelve, and
          this guy comes up. And I notice
          because the whole thing seems kind
          of seedy. And then I see the guy
          give the kid some money and they
          disappear down under the underpass.

                    MARTIN
          And then what happened?

                    WITNESS
          Well, I couldn't believe it, a kid that
          age turning tricks, so when he comes up
          a few minutes later, I ask him if he's
          got parents somewhere.
                    (MORE)

                                          (CONTINUED)

28   CONTINUED: 28

                                   WITNESS (cont'd)
                         You know what he says? He asks me if I
                         want a...date. I'll never forget it as   *
                         long as I live. Then I go home later and
                         I turn on the TV and there's the kid.
                         The "Birthday Boy".

                                   MARTIN
                         And you're sure it was him?

                                   WITNESS
                         You don't forget something like
                         that.

                                   MARTIN
                         He was wearing a very distinctive
                         jacket. Do you remember that?

                                   WITNESS
                              (vague)
                         It was kind of funky. You know, one
                         of these jackets the teenagers
                         wear. With some kind of logo or
                         something on it.

Martin shows him a picture.

                                   MARTIN
                         Is this it?

                                   WITNESS
                         Yeah yeah, that's it. Definitely.

                                   MARTIN
                         You're absolutely certain?

                                   WITNESS
                         No question. I told you, you don't
                         forget something like that.

Martin sighs, flips the picture on his desk, frustrated. And
now we see it: the jacket Martin's just shown him looks
nothing like Gabe's "Thrash Dog" jacket. He rolls his eyes,
pissed off.

                                   MARTIN
                         Get the hell out of here.

29   EXT.   WEST 40'S - SIMULTANEOUS   29

An eclectic mix of funky/tough-looking/mixed ethnic Teens and
Pre-teens skateboard feverishly up and around the ramps and
loading docks of abandoned warehouses.

ANGLE ON Danny and Jack with WALLY, 13, tough, street-smart:

                                                          (CONTINUED)

Without A Trace Episode #1 "Birthday Boy" (Pink) 7/19/02   28.

29   CONTINUED: 29

                        WALLY
              I didn't call 'cause I didn't think
              I had nothing to say.

                        DANNY
              You didn't think him being here the
              night he disappeared might be
              useful to us?

                        WALLY
              I figured you's knew that already.

                        JACK
              It's all right, Wally. We get it.
              Just tell us about that night. You
              remember about what time he showed
              up here?

                        WALLY
              I didn't get here 'til about seven
              and I guess it was a bit after   *
              that.   *

                        JACK
              ...about seven-thirty?   *

                        WALLY
              Yeah probably. He comes up acting   *
              all phat-like 'cause he's got some
              money in his pocket...

29A   **EXT. WEST 40'S - EVENING**   29A

**Gabe appears and we are BACK IN TIME (circa 7:30 DOD). His
NY cap is now turned backward and he has a street strut we
haven't seen before. His whole persona is faux
tough/braggadocio:**

                        GABE
              What up, dogs?
                  (flashing his money)
              Check what I got.

                        WALLY
              **Where'd you get that? You mug an
              old lady?**

A couple of the other kids laugh.

                        GABE
              **I ditched my old man on the subway
              and scalped my ticket.**

                                                      (CONTINUED)

29A   CONTINUED: 29A

                        BONES   *
            You trippin', man. He's gonna whoop
            your ass.

                        GABE
            Yeah, whatever. Who's got a board
            for me?

        Someone flips him an extra board. Gabe catches it with one   *
        hand, drops it to the ground, expertly hops aboard, rides it
        up a curb and FADES AWAY...

29B   EXT.   WEST 40'S - SIMULTANEOUS - RESUMING   29B

                        JACK
            So then what?

                        WALLY
            Not much. He hung out a few hours,
            'til like nine, nine-thirty, then
            we took off.

                        DANNY
            He say where he was going?

                        WALLY
            Home, I think. We figured his dad
            was gonna smoke him, but he wasn't
            sweatin' it.

                        JACK
            Did he mention that it was his
            birthday?

                        WALLY
            Nah. I didn't hear about that 'til
            I saw it in the news. That's kind
            of whack, huh?

30   INT.   FBI OFFICE - 11 AM (41 HOURS MISSING)   30

           TIMELINE SHOT: 7:30 - 9:30 - Boarding - West Side

           Martin, on the phone, sticks yet another pin in the map of
           "Gabe Sightings." ND Agent hands Martin a slip of paper,   *
           puts up two fingers as in - "line two."   *

                        MARTIN
            Right, well thank you. We
            appreciate your help.

                                                        (CONTINUED)

30   CONTINUED: 30

Martin hangs up, sighs, looks at the paper, scoops up the   *
phone.

                         MARTIN (CONT'D)   *
             Fitzgerald...Right...Right...At   *
             Port Authority?...Okay,   *
             when?...Right, do you remember what
             color the jacket was?

Martin's face changes from skepticism to hope.

                         MARTIN (cont'd)
             And the sleeves?

Hope to optimism.

                         MARTIN (cont'd)
             How about the logo?

Optimism to excitement.

                         MARTIN (cont'd)
             And you say this was ten minutes ago?

31   INT. PORT AUTHORITY - 11:20 AM   31

Port Authority Police scattered all over the place, hungrily
searching for Gabe. There are a lot of teenagers and pre-
teens. Some look like runaways, others look homeless, others
just look like tough kids who hang out here.

ANGLE ON Danny and Jack looking together.

ANGLE ON Samantha and Vivian across the way, desperately
looking for Gabe.

Suddenly, Samantha spots him fifty yards away, walking with a
GIRL about his height:

                         SAMANTHA
                   (into her walkie-cell
                   phone)
             We got him near the concourse.

Danny and Jack hurry over. Samantha and Vivian move in, too.

                         SAMANTHA (cont'd)
             Gabe!...Gabe!

(CONTINUED)

31   CONTINUED: 31

But he keeps moving, all we see is the "Thrash Dog" insignia
on the back of his jacket. Finally, Samantha catches up,
grabs him. He turns, pissed, and we realize it's not him.

                    GIRL
          What the hell's your problem, lady?

                    SAMANTHA
          We're FBI, don't go anywhere.

ANGLE ON Jack and Danny rushing over excitedly. Their faces
change to disappointment when they arrive and realize...

The KID is eleven or twelve -- tough, unkempt, unwashed.
Probably homeless. And not Gabe.

                    JACK
          Where'd you get that jacket?

                    KID
          What do you mean? It's mine.

                    JACK
          Get it off him.

Samantha wrestles it off him as the Girl lunges for her.

                    GIRL
          Leave him alone!

Danny grabs the Girl, pulls her back. Jack helps Samantha
get hold of the Kid so they can look at the jacket. She
finally gets it off, checks the label.   *

                    SAMANTHA
          It's Gabe's.   *

Vivian grabs a sleeve, looks at it closely.

                    VIVIAN
          Jack...there's dried blood on the sleeve.

Jack looks, as we PUSH IN ON the bloody sleeve...

                    END ACT TWO

ACT THREE

32   INT.   PORT AUTHORITY - 12 PM (42 HOURS MISSING)   32

The Kid (named LEO) looks extremely distressed as he shows
Jack and Danny:

>   LEO
>   I swear to God, I found the jacket
>   right there. In the garbage. I
>   never saw him.

>   DANNY
>   And you didn't notice the blood?

>   LEO
>   (lying)
>   I didn't know what the hell it was.
>   I thought it might be paint or
>   something.

>   JACK
>   Was it already dry?

>   LEO
>   Yeah.

>   JACK
>   You're sure?

>   LEO
>   It would've gotten on my hand.

Vivian comes over. Jack meets her.

>   VIVIAN
>   Leo's "girlfriend" corroborates his
>   story.

>   JACK
>   She confirm the time?

>   VIVIAN
>   Four A.M.
>   (pointing to bar across
>   way)
>   She remembers because the diner
>   was just closing.
>   (shifting gears)
>   I ran Leo's name. Turns out his
>   mother reported him missing eight
>   months ago out of Baltimore.
>   Abusive stepfather.

                                        (CONTINUED)

32   CONTINUED: 32

> JACK   *
> What about the girl?
>
> VIVIAN
> She escaped from a foster home in Boston.
> No abuse, she says. Just neglect. Social   *
> Services is on their way.   *

Jack reacts: he's seen this all before, looks back at Leo.   *

33   INT. FBI COMMAND POST - 1 PM   33

The team assembled. Vivian debriefing:

> VIVIAN
> NYPD is canvassing the ticket
> agents, vendors, janitors, but so
> far, nothing.   *

Jack gets up, moves to the TIMELINE:

> JACK
> We know he scalped his ticket at
> seven, took a train down to the
> West 40's, hung out there until
> nine, nine-thirty. And then the
> bloody jacket turns up at four AM
> at Port Authority. Question is,
> how'd the jacket get there and why?
>
> SAMANTHA
> Maybe he was running away. Maybe
> that's what this is about.
>
> JACK
> From what?
>
> DANNY
> Maybe he was running to something.
> Or someone.

(CONTINUED)

33   CONTINUED: 33

> MARTIN
> You can't get too far with fifty bucks.   *
>
> DANNY
> You don't know how much allowance
> he already had in his pocket.
>
> SAMANTHA
> Just because the jacket was there
> doesn't mean he was.
>
> MARTIN
> No, but maybe he was in the vicinity.   *

Martin moves to the map with all the pins in it.

> MARTIN (cont'd)
> We've got three sightings in that
> ten block radius. A movie theater,
> a diner, and a cyber-café. But the
> cyber-cafe's the only sighting that   *
> fits our timeline. And this place
> was busted last month for letting
> under-age kids have access to porn.
>
> JACK
> Samantha, why don't you check that out?

Martin is a bit stung but knows he's being hazed.   And
Samantha notices.

> DANNY
> We don't know he ever made it   *
> anywhere near Port Authority. For
> all we know, those boarders ripped
> off his fifty bucks, killed him and
> dumped his jacket at Port
> Authority.   *

An Agent hands Jack a file.   He looks it over.

> JACK
> Forensics. The blood on the jacket's
> O positive. Same as Gabe's.

The room takes that in.   Then...

(CONTINUED)

33   CONTINUED: (2)   33

> JACK (cont'd)
> (short-hand orders to
> Samantha, Vivian, Danny)
> Cyber-café, Port Authority,
> skateboarders...

He turns to Martin but Martin beats him to the punch.

> MARTIN
> Office.

> JACK
> (heading out)
> I'll go see the parents.

34   INT. FREEDMAN APARTMENT - LIVING ROOM - 2 PM (44 HOURS   34
      MISSING)

Dale and Bob clutch hands, sitting next to one another, their
worst nightmare slowly coming true. Jack stands.

> JACK
> We won't know for sure it's his
> blood until we do a DNA test.

They look at each other: this is awful.

> BOB
> So what do you need?

> JACK
> His toothbrush. Or a comb.

A beat. That hangs in the air. Awful. Then Dale gets up to
go get it. And her knees buckle. Bob reaches for her. She
steadies herself and exits the room.

Jack and Bob share a look.

35   EXT. WEST 48TH STREET - 2 PM (44 HOURS MISSING)   35

Danny with Wally hanging out in his usual spot. Vince and
Bones looking on warily, from a distance.

> DANNY
> (a bit street)   *
> I'm not a cop, all right? I don't give a
> damn about what you're into. I gotta find
> your friend, that's it. So if you care
> about him at all, you've got to be
> straight with me.

Wally eyes Vince and Bones.

(CONTINUED)

35   CONTINUED: 35

                         DANNY (cont'd)
              Hey, I'm not gonna make you a rat,
              all right?
                   (in Spanish)
              This is just between me and you,   *
              that's it.

                         WALLY
              I wasn't there when it happened so
              I don't know too much, all right?

                         DANNY
              When what happened?

                         WALLY
              They all went to have some fun with   *
              one of the Koreans.

                         DANNY
              What Koreans?

                         WALLY
              You know, one of the delis. I don't
              know which. They went to mess with
              the guy or somethin'.

                         DANNY
              What do you mean "mess with"?

                         WALLY
              Nothin' serious, man. They're
              stupid. That's why I don't even run
              with that. They go in there and
              lift a bag of chips or somethin',   *
              it's stupid.

                         DANNY
              And Gabe was with them?

                         WALLY
              I told him not to go, but -- I
              guess it got kind of out of hand or
              somethin'. I don't really know.

Danny looks where Vince and Bones were standing. They're
gone now, though some others stay. Danny grabs Wally's wrist
hard.

                         DANNY
              Push me away.
                   (off Wally's startled
                   look)
                        (MORE)

                                                        (CONTINUED)

35   CONTINUED: (2)   35

> DANNY (cont'd)
> Push me away so they know you're
> not a rat.

35   CONTINUED: (3)   35

Wally pushes him.

36   INT. CYBER-CAFE - SIMULTANEOUS   36

CYBER GUY warily hands Gabe's picture back to Samantha.

                         CYBER GUY
               You're not gonna run me in for this?

                         SAMANTHA
               I just need the information.

                         CYBER GUY
               Yeah, he was here that night, he
               came in around 11:30...

36A   **INT. CYBER-CAFE - NIGHT**   36A

**Gabe appears, entering the Cafe and we are BACK IN TIME
(11:30 PM DOD). He looks distressed, trying to hold it
together, as he approaches the counter.**

                         GABE
               **I need to use one of your
               computers.**

                         CYBER GUY
                    **(points to the "No One
                    Under 16..." sign)**
               Can't do it.

                         GABE
               Please. Just five minutes. Please.   *

Cyber Guy hesitates, looks around.   *

                         CYBER GUY   *
               Go ahead.   *

As Gabe heads to the computers, he fades away.

36B   INT. CYBER-CAFE - SIMULTANEOUS - RESUMING   36B

Cyber Guy turns back to Samantha and we are in the PRESENT.

                         CYBER GUY
               It wasn't five minutes, though. He
               logged on, looked like he sent one
               email, then just sat there staring
               at the screen, not doing much of
               anything for maybe half an hour.
                         (MORE)

                                                        (CONTINUED)

36B   CONTINUED: 36B

                              CYBER GUY (cont'd)
                    Then all of a sudden, he starts
                    typing away like crazy.

                              SAMANTHA
                    Did he have blood on his jacket?

                              CYBER GUY
                    Not that I saw.

                              SAMANTHA
                    Which computer was he on?

37   INT. FBI OFFICE - 2:30 PM (44.5 HOURS MISSING)   37

      Martin on the phone.

                              MARTIN
                    I checked all the logs. There was no
                    violent crime reported in that area
                    the night of the disappearance.

      INTERCUT with:

38   EXT. DOWNTOWN STREET - SIMULTANEOUS   38

      Danny on the corner, on his cell.

                              DANNY
                    On a Friday night. Are you sure?

                              MARTIN
                    Yes I'm sure. I even ran Chelsea and the
                    West Village. Nothing in the time period
                    we're looking at.

                              DANNY
                    Damn.

                              MARTIN
                    I did, however, check with local
                    hospitals. A Korean Deli Owner
                    checked himself into the E.R. at
                    St. Vincent's around eleven PM.
                    Head wounds.

                              DANNY
                    Why didn't you say that in the
                    first place?

                              MARTIN
                    Because you never told me you were
                    looking for a Korean Deli Owner. I
                    had to hear that from Jack.

                                                    (CONTINUED)

38   CONTINUED: 38

A long beat. Neither giving in.

                    MARTIN (cont'd)
              You want the address?

39   INT. KOREAN DELI - 3 PM (45 HOURS MISSING)   39

DELI OWNER, with bandage on his head and thick accent, tells
Danny what happened that night:

                    DELI OWNER
              I'm here just doing business and
              they come in with their skateboard
              and making trouble. It's not right.
              I would call police but they don't
              do anything.

                    DANNY
              I understand. Just tell me what
              happened.

Deli Owner takes a sip of his drink.

                    DELI OWNER
              They come in, over there...

He points to the door on the right and...

39A   **INT. KOREAN DELI - NIGHT**   39A

**Gabe appears with his Boarding Friends, looking for a little
mischief. We are BACK IN TIME (10 PM DOD). The friends hang
back. Gabe steps forward, friends watching him closely, as
if this is a hazing thing. He comes forward tentatively,
clearly doesn't want to do this. Deli Owner eyes him, eyes
the others. Suddenly, Gabe grabs a bag of chips and dashes
for the door. His friends, positioned conveniently near the
door, race out ahead of him. Gabe trips over a broom. Deli
Owner gives chase from around the counter and grabs him.
Gabe tries to wrestle himself free and in the struggle they
fall against the wall of liquor bottles. One falls off the
top and smashes Deli Owner in the head.**

**DELI OWNER'S POV -- Getting woozy as a fuzzy image of Gabe
leans over him and then BLACKNESS...**

40   OMITTED   40

41   OMITTED   41

Without A Trace Episode #1 "Birthday Boy" (Goldenrod) 7/30/02   40.

42   INT.   KOREAN DELI - 3 PM (45 HOURS MISSING) - RESUMING   42

                            DELI OWNER
                I wake up later and go hospital. I
                nearly died.

                            DANNY
                That's probably what he thought.

                            DELI OWNER
                He didn't call help or nothing.

                            DANNY
                He must've been scared.

                            DELI OWNER
                Stupid kids. What you do in this
                country with your kids?

43   INT.   PORT AUTHORITY - INFORMATION BOOTH - SIMULTANEOUS   43   *

        Info Guy looks at a photo of Gabe, doesn't recognize him,   *
        hands it to his cohort JOHNNY.   *

                            JOHNNY
                Yeah sure, I remember this kid.   *
                He was here Friday night, looking   *
                to buy a ticket...   *

43A   INT.   PORT AUTHORITY - INFORMATION BOOTH - NIGHT   43A   *

        Gabe appears at the counter and we're BACK IN TIME (circa
        Midnight, DOD).

                            GABE
                Excuse me, where do I buy a bus ticket?   *

                            JOHNNY   *
                Depends where you're going.   *

                            GABE   *
                Texas.   *

                            JOHNNY   *
                This ticket for you?   *

                            GABE   *
                Yeah.   *

                                                      (CONTINUED)

43A   CONTINUED: 43A

                              JOHNNY   *
                    You've got to be at least fifteen. And   *
                    to go across the state line, you've got
                    to have a note from your parents. Or be
                    accompanied by an adult.

          Gabe, disappointed, fades away...

43B   INT. PORT AUTHORITY - INFORMATION BOOTH - RESUMING   43B   *

                              JOHNNY
                    I don't know what happened to him   *
                    after that.   *

                              VIVIAN
                    An eleven year old wandering around
                    here by himself at midnight, trying
                    to get to Texas, why didn't you
                    call a cop?

                              JOHNNY
                    Hey, kids like that come here   *
                    every day.

44   INT. FBI - COMMAND POST - 3:30 PM (45.5 HOURS MISSING)   44

          Samantha makes her way over to Jack.

                              SAMANTHA
                    We got the email he sent from the
                    Cyber-Café. You ready for this?
                         (reading text off a page)
                    "Dad, I really messed up and I'm in
                    big trouble. Please email me when
                    you sign on. I'm waiting."

                              JACK
                    And what was the response?

                              SAMANTHA
                    We don't know. There were some Instant-
                    Messages but we can't read them.

          A long beat. Jack doesn't get it.

                              JACK
                    Dad?

                              SAMANTHA
                         (handing him the paper)
                    Dad.

(CONTINUED)

Without A Trace Episode #1 "Birthday Boy" (Pink) 7/19/02   42.

44   CONTINUED: 44

END ACT THREE

ACT FOUR

45   INT. FREEDMAN APARTMENT - LIVING ROOM - 4PM (46 HOURS   45
MISSING)

Jack and Samantha sit with Bob and Dale. Samantha doing most
of the talking, Jack watching the father like a hawk.

                  SAMANTHA
          The Deli Owner passed out for at
          least half an hour. It was his
          blood on the jacket. Gabe must've
          thought he'd killed him. He didn't
          know what to do. So now he walks
          the streets, tries to get a hold of
          himself, figure out a plan, and
          finally, a couple of hours later,
          he heads for Port Authority. When
          he saw the blood on his jacket, he
          panicked and threw it in the
          garbage.

                  DALE
          Oh my God. Port Authority?

                  SAMANTHA
          He tried to buy a bus ticket to   *
          somewhere in Texas.

Bob and Dale look at each other.

                  BOB
          Texas?

                  DALE
           We don't know anyone in Texas.

                  BOB
           You said <u>tried</u>. He <u>tried</u> to buy a ticket?

                  SAMANTHA
          He's too young, so they wouldn't   *
          sell him one. We think maybe he   *
          asked someone at Port Authority to
          buy a ticket for him. We're
          checking all children's tickets
          bought during that twelve hour
          period.

                  DALE
          This doesn't make sense. Why
          wouldn't he call us if he got into
          trouble?

                                      (CONTINUED)

45   CONTINUED: 45

                              SAMANTHA
                    That's what we were trying to figure
                    out. Until we found the email.

JACK'S POV - Bob's expression: surprise.

                              DALE
                    What email?

                              JACK
                    The one he sent your husband.

Dale looks at Bob. Bob looks at Jack.

                              BOB
                    What the hell are you talking
                    about?

                              JACK
                    He sent you an email. Asking for help.

                              BOB
                    This is insane, this is absolutely
                    insane. You think I was emailing my
                    son in the middle of the night?
                    After all of this, you think I know
                    where he is? You people are
                    unbelievable!

Dale on the other side of the room, not sure what to make of
this. Does she still trust her husband?

                              BOB (CONT'D)
                    I wasn't even on the computer that
                    night! You were here.

                              DALE
                         (confused)
                    I don't remember. I can't remember.

                              JACK
                    We understand you didn't want your
                    son to get into trouble. And the
                    Deli Owner's fine. He's not going
                    to press charges.

                              BOB
                    I swear to God, this is the
                    Twilight Zone. I haven't seen or
                    heard from my son in two days!

                                                      (CONTINUED)

Without A Trace Episode #1 "Birthday Boy" (Pink) 7/19/02   45.

45   CONTINUED: (2)   45

> SAMANTHA
> Well whoever he was communicating
> with, he was calling him "Dad."   *

> DALE
> Oh my God....Oh my God.

They look at her: a horrible epiphany hitting her like a
freight train.

> DALE (cont'd)
> He found him. Oh my God, he found him.

> BOB
> (totally confused)
> Who?!

Dale looks at Bob.   *

> JACK
> (dawning on him)
> His father. His birth father.

Samantha looks quizzically at Jack: what's going on here?

> JACK (CONT'D)
> Gabe's adopted, isn't he?

Dale nods through her tears. Bob goes to her.

> SAMANTHA
> Why didn't you tell us this from
> the beginning?

Bob and Dale look at each other. Even they don't know.

> DALE
> He's our son, he's been our son
> since his second day of life. We've
> never thought of him any other way.
> My poor baby.

> BOB
> (to Dale)
> How could he have found out?

> JACK
> You never told him?

> DALE
> We were going to wait until he was
> older. We thought he'd be able to
> handle it better.

(CONTINUED)

45   CONTINUED: (3)   45

                              BOB
                    I don't understand. You're saying
                    he's been communicating over the
                    internet with his biological
                    father? And then he gets into
                    trouble and he goes to him? Not us?

                              JACK
                    He doesn't trust you right now. You
                    lied to him. As far as he's
                    concerned, you've lied to him his
                    whole life. That's why he's been
                    acting this way for the past four
                    months. That's why he reacted that
                    way to his birthday at school.
                    That's why he didn't want to go to
                    the game with you.

                              BOB
                    We don't even know who -- who his
                    "father" is.

46   INT. ADOPTION AGENCY OFFICE - 4:30 PM (46.5 HOURS MISSING)46

A cramped old office. Middle-aged, over-worked, harried
DOLORES looks at the adoption papers, combs through mounds of
files in a huge filing cabinet. Vivian stands by the desk,
waiting for help.

                              DOLORES
                    He couldn't have found the kid
                    through us. We don't give out that
                    information. Not without consent of
                    the adoptive parents.

                              DANNY
                    Maybe he hacked into your computer.

                              DOLORES
                    Anything before 1994 never got
                    inputted into the computer.

                              VIVIAN
                    Well we'd appreciate your help.

                                                    (CONTINUED)

46   CONTINUED: 46

                              DOLORES
                    I'm sorry, but we need to protect
                    the anonymity of our clients.

                              DANNY
                    Look, Mrs. Canon, you can help us
                    now or you can wait another hour or
                    two 'til we get that court order.
                    You help us now, maybe we save this
                    kid and maybe you get home to your
                    family in time for dinner.

         Dolores hesitates.

46A   INT. ADOPTION AGENCY - MOMENTS LATER   46A

         Dolores sits behind her desk with the file in front of her
         now. Vivian and Danny looking on expectantly.

                              DOLORES
                    Gabe Freedman. Biological mother:
                    Barbara Young, lives in San
                    Francisco. Biological father:
                    Edward Perkins...<u>died</u> three years   *
                    ago.

         Danny and Vivian look at each other.

                              DANNY
                    Then who's he running to?

47   INT. FBI OFFICE - COMMAND POST - 5 PM (47 HOURS MISSING) 47

         Jack, Samantha, Martin, Danny, Vivian:

                              SAMANTHA
                    So far, all we got on that email   *
                    address is that it's registered in
                    Texas.

                              JACK
                    That doesn't give us much. We
                    already know that's where he's
                    headed.

                              DANNY
                    So you're thinking some friend,
                    some family member, maybe someone
                    at the adoption agency, knew Gabe
                    was adopted, broke the news to him
                    over the internet, has been using
                    that information to prey on him and
                    has now lured him to Texas?

                                              (CONTINUED)

47   CONTINUED: 47

                          SAMANTHA
          Right.

(CONTINUED)

47   CONTINUED: (2)   47

                    DANNY
          But why would they think that could
          work? If Gabe didn't even know he was
          adopted? Why would he believe them?

                    JACK
          Maybe they had a copy of the
          records. Maybe they know about that
          birthmark on his right shoulder.
          Maybe they just preyed on the
          insecurities every kid has when a
          new baby enters the family.

                    SAMANTHA
          Either way, they convinced him and
          managed to con him into not telling
          his parents.

                    VIVIAN
          They found him four or five months
          ago. That would explain his change
          in behavior at school...

                    SAMANTHA
          And his reaction to that birthday
          party.

The phone buzzes. Samantha picks it up.   *

                    JACK
          The first contact must have been
          through email but since then, it's
          been all Instant Message. Which is
          why none of their communication
          showed up on Gabe's computer.   *

Samantha puts the phone on hold.   *

                    SAMANTHA   *
          John Scarparelli, from Greyhound.   *

Vivian moves off to take the call in her cubicle.   *

                    MARTIN
          Isn't it possible that Gabe found
          out he was adopted? And he's the
          one who initiated all of this?
               (shows paper to Jack)
          There are all of these find-your-
          parent, find-your-child websites.
          Most of them aren't regulated, any
          John Q.
                    (MORE)

                                          (CONTINUED)

47   CONTINUED: (3)   47

                              MARTIN (cont'd)
               Pedophile who wants to lure kids to
               his lair puts one of these on the
               net and he's in business.

                                                           (CONTINUED)

47   CONTINUED: (4)   47

                          DANNY
              That makes more sense to me.

                          MARTIN
              I ran background checks on all of
              these websites. One of them's
              registered in Amarillo, Texas.

Vivian comes over, having just finished her call.

                          VIVIAN
              One adult ticket, one child's
              ticket purchased at one-thirty AM
              the night of the disappearance. But
              not to Texas. To Santa Fe.

                          DANNY
              Some little old lady buys him a
              ticket, escorts him on the bus,
              thinks she's doing him a favor.

                          JACK
              Santa Fe. That's three hundred
              miles from Amarillo.

                          SAMANTHA   *
              If you're Gabe, Santa Fe's a lot
              closer than New York.

                          JACK
              When does that bus get in?

                          VIVIAN
              Twenty minutes ago.   *

                          JACK
              Call the regional office right
              away.

As Vivian goes, Jack to the rest of the group:

                          JACK (CONT'D)
              So if you're Gabe, what do you do now?

                          MARTIN
              Get back on the net. See what "Dad" says.

48   INT. FBI COMPUTER ROOM - 5:10 PM (47.2 HOURS MISSING)   48

A TECH on a computer, monitoring accounts of "Dad" and Gabe.
Jack and Martin sitting on counter nearby.

                                                    (CONTINUED)

48   CONTINUED: 48

> JACK
> You got anything more on the
> pedophile's email address?
>
> TECH
> We've narrowed it down to Amarillo.

(CONTINUED)

48   CONTINUED: (2)   48

Jack looks at Martin: you were right.

> MARTIN   *
> So the pervert starts a website
> where he pretends to help adopted
> kids find their natural parents.
> The kids log on, give their names,
> ask for help. He goes along,
> pretends to do all the research,
> then tells the kid, "I found your
> father. Here's his email address."

> JACK
> Right. But it's his own address.
> The kid contacts him, he pretends
> to be surprised, then he tells the
> kid to communicate only by Instant
> Message. "That way no one will
> know. It'll be our secret."

> MARTIN
> And then he lures them in. Sick
> bastard.

> JACK   *
> In all likelihood, he's just your   *
> Average Joe. A job, a life, the guy   *
> next door.   *

> TECH
> Gotta hit.

They look over at that screen: the "Dad" is on.

> TECH (CONT'D)
> Here we go. We got the kid.

"Gabe" is now logged on.

INSERT COMPUTER SCREEN 1: "Dad, it's me."

They look toward other computer:

INSERT COMPUTER SCREEN 2: "Where are you? I'm waiting for
you."

Jack and Martin share a look: here we go.

Without A Trace Episode #1 "Birthday Boy" (Pink) 7/19/02   51.

49   INT.   FBI COMMAND POST - MOMENTS LATER   49

Jack bounds in, Martin on his heels. The others look up from
their CUBICLES:

                    JACK
          Gabe's staying put in Santa Fe. "Dad"'s
          driving out to meet him. If we hop on the
          next plane, we should just beat him
          there. Viv, let Santa Fe know I'm on my
          way. Sam, call the family. Danny, you
          come with me.

They head out. Jack turns back.

                    JACK (cont'd)
          Martin. You, too.

Martin goes. Samantha looks after them.   *

50   EXT. SANTA FE AIRPORT - STOCK SHOT   50

Plane landing. Dusk/Night.

51   EXT.   MUNICIPAL PARK - 9:15 PM (51.25 HOURS MISSING)   51

Jack and Martin fanning out into stakeout position.

                    JACK
          Sometimes I wish I never quit
          smoking.
               (into radio)
          Any sign of the boy?

                    RADIO VOICE 1
          South Entrance, negative.

ANGLE ON Danny near the SNACK BAR, a female agent on his arm.

                    RADIO VOICE 2
          Snack Bar, negative.

ANGLE ON Martin passing a Tall Man on the walkway, trying to
read his face. Is this the guy?

Danny takes a seat with his female agent, pretending to be
romantic, on a PARK BENCH. A Bald Man sitting on a bench
opposite him reads the PAPER beneath a lamppost.

Jack gazes all around the PARK, trying to take it all in.

Danny spots a figure emerging from the TREEHOUSE atop the
JUNGLE GYM.

                                        (CONTINUED)

51   CONTINUED: 51

                          DANNY
                     (into radio)
                 Possible ID on the boy. Coming from
                 the jungle gym.

                          JACK
                     (into radio)
                 Hold your position.

The figure from the TREEHOUSE emerges.   It's Gabe.

A PARK MAINTENANCE GUY emptying the garbage pauses, whispers
into his cuff.

                     PARK MAINTENANCE GUY
                 I've got the boy.

                          JACK
                     (into radio)
                 Move in range, but do not seize. Do
                 not seize.

Danny inches closer.   Martin creeps in, too.

The Man with the PAPER looks around for a moment, glances in
the direction of Gabe, gets up, tucks the paper under his arm.

                          DANNY
                     (into radio)
                 Bald man with newspaper heading
                 north. Toward the boy.

Gabe looks around, nervous, scared.   Sees Bald Man coming
toward him.

                     PARK MAINTENANCE GUY
                 The boy's within range. Should we grab
                 him?

Jack on a HILL, can see everything beneath him, like chess
pieces on a board.

                          JACK
                 Hold your position. You've got five
                 more seconds.

Jack looks around.   Sees another man, a new figure, heading
across the grass from a distance.

                     PARK MAINTENANCE GUY
                 Gotta go here, Jack.

                                              (CONTINUED)

Without A Trace Episode #1 "Birthday Boy" (Pink) 7/19/02   52A.

51   CONTINUED: (2)   51

                          JACK
          Wait.

(CONTINUED)

51   CONTINUED: (3)   51

Bald Man swerves suddenly out of his path, apparently toward
Gabe.

                    PARK MAINTENANCE GUY
              Suspect confirmed. Moving in!

They converge on him quickly.   *

                    PARK MAINTENANCE GUY (cont'd)
              FBI! Get down on the ground!   *

A cacophony of voices, including Danny sprinting in as the   *
Bald Man drops to the ground, stunned.   *

Gabe freaking out: *

                    GABE
              Dad? Is that you?

But Jack is fixated on: the FIGURE heading toward them in   *
the grass, who suddenly turns and does an about-face.

                    JACK
                 (into radio)
              Hold the perimeter! Hold the
              perimeter!

But it's too late as Jack starts to give chase. And now the
Figure is picking up his pace. And when he senses Jack
behind him, he takes off.

Jack runs, pulls his gun.

                    JACK (cont'd)
                 (into radio)
              Seal the exits. Suspect running west.

                    DANNY
                 (into radio)
              We've got him!

                    JACK
                 (into radio)
              No you don't!

ANGLE ON Martin running through the park.

Jack chasing the Figure.

                    JACK (cont'd)
                 (into radio)
              He's cutting toward the lake!   *

                                                        (CONTINUED)

Drama Outline and Script | 195

51   CONTINUED: (4)   51

Martin swerves toward the LAKE. The Figure races by. Martin
comes at him, tackles him into the LAKE.

Jack arrives, out of breath, sees Martin with a firm hold on
the guy, dragging him out of the LAKE.

Jack moves toward him for support, training his gun on the
suspect. Other Agents emerge now, too. And the suspect is   *
surrounded. They drag him away.

Martin steps onto land.

                    JACK (cont'd)
          You learn that in white collar?

                    MARTIN
          Sixth grade swim class.

Jack, out of breath...

                    JACK
          I was gaining on him, you know.

                    MARTIN
                (a half smile)
          Right. Sorry about that.

52   INT. FBI OFFICE - DAWN   52

Samantha with Bob and Dale watch expectantly, anxiously.   *

                    SAMANTHA   *
          His name's Darin Oaks. He's a   *
          paralegal, he's married and he has   *
          two children. We know he's contacted   *
          other boys over the Internet but we   *
          think this is the first time he's   *
          tried anything like this.   *

Dale and Bob react. Vivian comes over.   *

                    VIVIAN   *
          Gabe's on his way up.   *

Dale and Bob breathe a sigh of relief. Allow themselves
smiles for the first time in days. Then, as they prepare,
Dale realizes what's imminently before her. She turns to Bob
and takes the responsibility on herself...

(CONTINUED)

Without A Trace Episode #1 "Birthday Boy" (Pink) 7/19/02   55.

52   CONTINUED: 52

                        SAMANTHA   *
             Just tell him what you told us.
             That you never thought of him as
             anything other than your own son.

                        BOB
             The truth is, I don't think we were
             protecting him. I think we were
             protecting ourselves.

                        VIVIAN
             Then tell him that.

53   INT. FBI ELEVATOR - SIMULTANEOUS   53

      Jack, Danny, Martin ride up with Gabe.

                        GABE
             So they know everything that
             happened?

                        JACK
             Everything we could tell them. You
             can fill them in on the rest.

                        GABE
             They're gonna kill me.   *

                        JACK
             No. They love you, Gabe.   *

                        GABE
             So if that wasn't my real father,
             then who is?

                        JACK
             Your parents can explain that a lot
             better than we can.

54   INT. FBI OFFICE - MOMENTS LATER   54

      Jack, Danny, Martin enter with Gabe. When Gabe sees his
      parents, he stops in his tracks. Dale rushes toward him,
      engulfs him in his arms, kisses him everywhere. Bob bends
      down, wraps them up in his, the three of them as one.

      Martin comes over to Samantha.

                        SAMANTHA
             Heard you got a little wet.

                                                         (CONTINUED)

Without A Trace Episode #1 "Birthday Boy" (Green) 7/29/02   56.

54   CONTINUED: 54

                           MARTIN
                It's better than sweating it out in   *
                the doghouse.   *

ANGLE ON Vivian and Danny. Danny sits down, exhausted at his
desk. Vivian comes over, drops a ticket on his desk.

Danny picks it up, looks at it.

                           VIVIAN
                The Red Sox in October.

Danny looks at her: okay, he puts it in his pocket. He'll
go with her.

Jack looks over at the family as they emerge from their hug,
wiping their eyes of tears. They walk off, Gabe between
them, one hand in each.

Jack goes over to the board, takes down Gabe's picture...

FADE OUT.

                          END ACT FOUR

Voices of Experience

10.

Advice from Industry Insiders

The inspiration behind our book is the enormous creative talent at Warner Bros. Television (WBTV). Among those most cherished are, of course, the writers. We asked several writers, either based at WBTV or alumni of the Warner Bros. Television Writers Workshop, for their perspective on how they got started and what they look for in new writers coming into the business. Their responses were insightful, honest, and often quite humorous.

John Beck
Workshop Alum—Class of 1996
Syracuse University Alum
Supervising Producer, *According to Jim*

Why did you choose to become a TV writer?
Okay, this is going to sound incredibly hokey, but I guess I knew from a very young age that I wanted to work in the entertainment industry in some capacity. After graduating from Syracuse University and moving to Hollywood, I had the always-hated task ahead of me of sorting through old, saved attic crap from years of elementary, junior high, high school, and college memories. You know what I'm talking about, con-

struction paper *Mayflowers*, old term papers on "Sounder," seeds pasted to poster board and pictures of what they'll grow into. (Much different seeds from second grade compared to college, I must say, though.) Anyway, as I sorted through crap, chucking this, chucking that, I came across a workbook my class had made in kindergarten—the "All about Me" book or something equally kindergarten-y. Inside were a series of pictures I had drawn of "what I would look like in twenty years" (oddly enough, like Han Solo—who knew?), "what my house would look like in twenty years" (nope, no giant birdcage on the roof), and "what your job will be when you grow up." I had drawn myself sitting in a director's chair, yelling through a megaphone and wearing the obligatory beret. Okay, Otto Preminger jokes aside, I thought that was pretty cool.

In high school I had always wanted to be an actor, and took that desire with me from my small little rural town to college at Syracuse, where I got to be around a lot of other really talented people who also had the acting bug in their small little rural towns. I got involved with the student TV station, UUTV, now HillTV, and sat in a room with these people and realized very quickly that without written material, you just had a bunch of funny people hanging out together and not much stuff being produced to be shot. So . . . someone had to write something. So I did. And people laughed. I had always been able to make people laugh while performing, but this was different. When someone new read it, they laughed then too. How great is that?! Anyone who has thought they were funny has been met with the blank stare that always seems to come when you retell a funny story that no longer makes sense because "you had to be there." You write it down—no more blank stares. You no longer "had to be there"! And more important, I had stuff I could perform.

So after graduation, now armed with my new skill, as well as with the Crayola-powered knowledge that I must be destined to work in the entertainment business, I packed all my worldly belongings in my crappy Ford Tempo and headed out west, determined to be a writer/actor. I dabbled in both for a bit, but finally went to my first audition and walked into the waiting area and saw fifty other guys who could have passed for me in a heartbeat. Same height, same weight, same hair color, same eye color, same desperation. I made the decision right then that I had to do something to differentiate myself from the masses. To have some more control. Creating gives you control. From that moment forward, I focused on writing—creating material—and haven't looked back. I still audition every once in a while for fun. But the cool thing with writing is you get to play every part in a script. Not just the one you are cast as.

What was your first sample script, and how did you get someone to read it?

Ron Hart, my writing partner whom I met at Syracuse and reconnected with out here in LA, and I struggled for years trying to get our break to become paid writers instead of the cute guys who really think "they are gonna make it in this business." Shows were cancelled, not renewed, not picked up, stars went insane, you name it. But we kept writing in the hopes that someone, somewhere, would read us and let us write for them. Finally, as an assistant on *The Hughleys*, one of the executive producers made the probably not-so-genuine offer to read one of our scripts—whiskey in the wrong hands can be a very valuable asset.

Anyway, I took him up on his offer and gave him our *Larry Sanders*, which he took home, and I waited. And waited. And waited. Day after day, he'd see my shining face and say, "Oh yeah. I got your script. It's sitting on my coffee table. I'm gonna get right on that." And then I'd wait. And wait. And wait. I also found out that another script made its way to his coffee table—this being one written by already established writers coming off a cancelled show. After a long weekend, the executive producer arrived one morning and told me that he had a funny evening at home the night before. He walked in to find his wife, who had also been in the entertainment business, reading the scripts that were sitting on the coffee table. She held it up and said, "Ugh. This script is awful. I hope you're not planning on hiring these guys." The executive producer then said to himself, "Man, I was really hoping Beck and Hart didn't suck. Good thing I put off reading their script so work didn't get awkward." His wife then held up the other script and said, "But these Beck and Hart guys . . . they're good. You should have them pitch." I was elated and waited for the offer to come in and pitch, but the executive producer just absentmindedly patted me on the back, told me he still hadn't gotten a chance to read our script, said I had a fan in his wife, and went into his office.

And so I waited. And waited. And waited. Each day he would come back in and say he was about to get to our script that night, and each following morning, he'd say he just didn't get around to it. I had written off our chances until Christmas vacation hit. I arrived to work after our break to find the executive producer waiting for me, saying Ron and I were going to come in and pitch. I asked if he liked my script. He said he still hadn't read it, but just spent two straight uninterrupted weeks with his wife nagging him as to when he was gonna bring us in.

We pitched. We sold the script. She got flowers. I love America.

What do you look for in a sample script today?
Funny jokes, interesting plot, and a compelling story. Now I know what you're saying: Aren't plot and story the same thing? No, they most certainly are not. The story is the conflict and resolution between two of your main characters. The plot is how that story plays out. There are a million different plots you can use to tell the same story, but regardless of how funny the plot is, if the story is lacking, the script will suffer.

Ron and I realized that after writing the first draft of our first sample script. We had hammered out a funny *NewsRadio*, and like the pesky assistants we were, we gave it to everyone we knew to read, ready to bask in their adulation. It didn't come. We got responses like: "It was funny, but I only got so far into it." "Nice. Keep working at it." "Yeah, nice jokes. Hey, shit-heel, I said no tomatoes on my sandwich."

So what was wrong? It made us laugh, but no one seemed to care about it. The answer? No story. Just plot. One of the writers, who was obviously much more patient and better at giving feedback, sat me down and explained that you need to have a strong conflict and through-line between two of your main characters. The plot is the series of situations that illustrate and complicate this basic story. I look at it now like curtains and curtain rods. The story is the rod that holds the curtains up. And no matter how beautiful these curtains are, they will be useless without the curtain rod.

Also, I look for how well the writer captures the voice of the series and that the story is set up in the first ten pages of the script.

What are the most common errors you find in sample material?
There are three common errors I find in the early careers of novice writers: waiting too long to set up a story, using too many outside characters, and trying to make a story from their lives fit into a series where it doesn't belong.

Your story should be set up in the first ten pages. When an executive, agent, or show runner is reading your script, he or she will have a stack of about three hundred to read. If he or she doesn't see that you know how to properly set up a story, it doesn't matter how good it gets; it's on to the next script. By the same token, you better have a great joke in the first three pages, if not on the first page. Strong scene blows are important too, because it makes the reader look forward to turning that page.

Many early writers use too many outside characters because they want to impress their reader with how funny a character is whom they created. Guess what? . . . Until you have created your own show, television writing is not about how well you can write your own material. It's about how well you can write someone else's material. Their characters, their point of view, and their style of writing. I know that sounds demeaning, but if you want to start creating your own characters, start writing screenplays. By the same token, don't create Man #1 and Man #2 to say something that Man #1 could say on his own, or even worse that one of your established characters could say.

The most common error I find in young writers is trying to make your favorite show do a story that happened to you. Always remember: Just because something was funny when it happened to you does not mean it will be funny when it happens to Chandler Bing. This doesn't mean that a story similar to the one that happened to you won't work with an established sitcom character. You just have to tailor it to make it fit the show's characters or sensibility. And by all means, don't create yourself as a character! I have read scripts written by aspiring writer/stand-ups that deal with Will and Grace running into a character named after themselves, and winced as page after page Will and Grace did nothing but comment on how funny their new friend is.

Remember, a sample script is what you do to show someone how well you can write their work.

Can you offer any tips or advice for anyone trying to break into television writing?
Writers write. Sounds stupid, but it's true. It's far too easy to say you are an up-and-coming writer yet never write anything.

You will hear all the time that it's all about being in the right place at the right time out in Hollywood. And while that is true, it is also just as true that you have to able to take advantage of a situation when you are in that place at the right time. You may spend years and years writing sample scripts and having no one read them. And then maybe you get frustrated with writing and slack off. Believe me, it's very easy in LA to decide to spend your weekend at the beach with your friends instead of cooped up in a dark little room coming up with funny shit for Raymond to say. But you need to put in the work. Because eventually someone's going to say, "Hey, I'd love to read your stuff," and you'll realize the last time you wrote anything, ALF was still in prime time. You were in the right place at the right time, but you didn't put yourself in the position to take advantage of it. On the flip side, make sure to go out, have fun, and do things because this is how you will meet the people you need to meet as well as come up with material to write about.

Always be good to the assistants. This is important to aspiring writers as well as working writers because the way this industry works, you never know whom you'll be working for five years down the road. "The toes you are stepping on today might very well be connected to the ass you need to be kissing tomorrow."

Ron Hart
Workshop Alum — Class of 1996
Syracuse Alum
Supervising Producer, *According to Jim*

Why did you choose to become a TV writer?
Somehow I figured out in high school that I wanted to study communications. At the time I think I wanted to be "talent" — an actor, or maybe a radio DJ. At Syracuse I got involved with the student television station. We produced a sitcom. I was a writer and helped out with the production stuff. I had a bit part that over the course of time became a regular character because I was getting laughs. Looking back on it, I was exactly the type of actor that I would hate to work with. I never knew my lines. I was horrible with doing anything physical, and I would constantly insert jokes that would allude to the fourth wall or refer to . . . well, my penis. One episode I had a joke about Culture Club so I came in dressed as Boy George. Just really hammy, upstagey, hacky crap. I noticed that I would almost never deliver my lines the way they were written because I thought I could make them better. I decided that meant I must be a better writer than actor. Truthfully, I was probably better at operating a boom mic than either of those jobs.

Anyway, I came out to LA right after graduation to get work in sitcoms. At the time the studios were handing out overall deals left and right, and kids who sold ad space on the *Harvard Lampoon* were getting recruited to be on the staffs of shows. I was under the impression that I merely had to move out here and wait for Hollywood to come knocking with a six-figure check to pay for my genius. It basically worked out that way . . . except that the wait was seven years.

What was your first sample script, and how did you get someone to read it?

I wrote a number of scripts by myself and with other writing partners before I started working with John Beck. We had been friends in college, but he was a few years behind me in school, so I had three years of failure and humiliation under my belt when he came out here. We thought we'd try writing together, and the first thing we wrote was a *NewsRadio*.

At the time I was working for a literary manager, Larry Shuman. I gave it to Larry to read and probably threatened to shred his financial files unless he did it that night. He liked it, but wasn't sure if that was just because he knew my personality. Meanwhile, we also submitted the script to the Warner Bros. Television Writers Workshop (we used the submission deadline as a motivator to get it done). Larry knew that the weeding-out process was pretty well regarded. When we were selected as finalists, he realized it wasn't just him and he signed us. We're still his clients today.

What do you look for in a sample script today?

I think it's so hard because there really isn't a show on the air right now that is really exceptional. Sometimes I read samples and think, "This could be the best episode of this show I've ever seen, but I hate this show." It makes it hard to be objective.

When I pick up a script, the first thing I look at is the formatting. I check the page count, eye the margins, make sure the spacing is right. It's superficial, but if they get that right it says to me this person is serious. They've either studied the format or they know it so well they don't have to.

Once I start reading, I look for a good joke. I think I do a good job of assuming a script will be funny until proven otherwise. If I start reading and there are obvious or tired jokes in the first couple pages, it causes me to mentally switch gears. A bad joke makes me think the writer is unfunny, and then I'm looking for further evidence of that and the good jokes won't make me laugh. I think the biggest mistake novices make with scripts is not putting blows at the end of scenes. Another trouble area is giving one character all the jokes and another character all the setup.

The accomplished writer/producer Ed Decter came to the Workshop when we were there and told us that Daphne had no attitude in our *Frasier* script. I reread it and realized we had only given her lines to set up our "brilliant" Niles jokes. When you're on a staff, you start thinking about those things because if an actor or actress is in a scene and doesn't have a clear line to play, you know that he or she will be in the writers' room the next day asking for something to do.

Structurally, I try to make sure that there is one salient story point in each scene. You want to see a story that builds over the course of the episode. It's really important to make the idea you're exploring in the story come through in the A scene. If they have a good act break, it's another sign that this is someone who understands the craft of sitcom.

And of course you want to make sure the writer captures the "voice" of the characters he or she is writing for. It's not just a matter of "that's more of a Joey joke than a Chandler joke"; it's about making sure the character doesn't go too far afield of what has been established by the series. The character is serving a purpose, is growing, but will be in the same state the writer found him or her in when the script began.

What are the most common errors you have found in sample scripts?

Here are some really red flags:

Crude humor. It's just so easy and fun to make fart and sex jokes. It's okay to be edgy, but you have to remember the format you're writing for. One of our scripts was a *Larry Sanders*. We loved being able to curse, but when we were through we read each joke and took out the word *fuck*. If it was still funny, we kept it in. If it wasn't, then we replaced it because we were just giggling at the curse word. The same can also be said for euphemisms for breasts, penises, farts, bowel movements, etc.

B-stories to nowhere. Usually writers spend the majority of their time crafting the A-story of their script. A B-story is very often a funny tangent that services the characters that you couldn't weave into the A-story. Very often this results in a situation where the characters in the B-story have no arc. Usually the joke is set up in the first pop, and then the scene just repeats itself with no real movement. I am always especially impressed when the tertiary story line intersects with the main story.

B-stories that are too good. Yes, the exact opposite happens. I've read a number of scripts where the B-story is better than the A-story. That really makes you wonder if that person is a good judge of story.

Scenes and/or acts that don't end with a strong joke.

A scene that seems to have no impact on the story.

A scene set in a location that is not a standing set that could have been told elsewhere.

A scene that is too long. Some shows, like *Everybody Loves Raymond*, do that, but in a sample it just makes it a hard read. Shorter scenes are always a better way to go.

Can you offer any tips or advice for anyone trying to break into television writing?

Go home. I need my fucking job, and I don't want some smart-ass twenty-three year old with four hundred times the energy I have turning into the next golden boy. Go write ad copy in New York. There's money in that, isn't there?

Oh. You're still here.

Fine. Don't come in with a chip on your shoulder. Everyone earns this job, one way or another. And don't think that just because someone wrote for *Full House*, they aren't funny. Judge writers on their writing, not their credits.

Don't be afraid to learn. This is not rocket science, but it ain't as easy as you think. You might be really funny, but you won't be the funniest person there. You might be 100 percent right about a fix to a scene, but you will be wrong. You might be there until midnight, but it's the best job in the world. So don't be an asshole to the PAs, and remember to thank whomever hired you each and every day.

And consider this: The field you're trying to break into is incredibly competitive. INCREDIBLY. There are more PROFESSIONAL FOOTBALL PLAYERS than there are writers who get paid to work on network sitcoms. The ONLY way you're going to get a job is to develop a personal relationship with a writer or executive who can hire you. Therefore, if you're a jerk . . . get a partner who can brownnose.

Remember that there are only a finite number of sitcoms on the air at any given time, and that means there are a finite number of jobs. As hard as it is to get your foot in the door as a sitcom writer, it's even harder to stay. Every time you move up a level in credit, you cut the number of jobs you're eligible for in half.

When you're uncredited and looking in, you're competing against everyone else that wants to get in. Once you're there and you're ready to move up to story editor, you're competing against everyone who's already at story editor, all the coproducers who haven't worked in two years and are taking a pay cut to get back in, plus all the other staff writers trying to move up. PLUS, each time you move up a rank, your pay goes up, and an executive producer looking at his writing budget has to think you're worth that much to him.

And then you have to keep moving up or else you'll get the reputation as someone who has plateaued, and people will assume you're either difficult to work with or not that talented.

Oh and by the way, not that you're ever going to have a real choice of what show you work on, but if you work on bad shows, you'll make less money, have less opportunities to develop, AND you'll have to prove yourself at each new job you go to.

Speaking of development, if you don't get a show on the air and into syndication, you'll most likely be looked at as someone who "couldn't create," even though you, in all likelihood, wrote a pilot that was really funny, but got noted to death by the network or was cast wrong. Regardless, you'll wind up having to take consulting jobs on shows run by people who were PAs when you were on top of the world, working with thirty year olds who think you're out of touch with reality, which is probably true because you don't want to be in touch with reality, but you have to keep working two more years to get your guild pension benefits.

If you break into this field and you find yourself sitting in a room with ten really funny people who are all trying to make each other laugh while a college graduate brings them lunch, don't mess it up. After all, it's the best job in the world.

Robert Borden
Executive Producer, *The George Lopez Show*

Why did you choose to become a TV writer?
Student loans.

What was the first script that you wrote, and how did you get someone to read it?
I wrote a *Simpsons*. A friend from college got it to an agent.

What do you look for in a sample script? What impresses you the most?
I look for a writer who can be funny in an original way, someone who can stand out. Like the Supreme Court justice said re: obscenity: "I know when I see it."

What are the most common errors you have found in sample scripts?
Usually the script is too long, the story too improbable, and the comedy too predictable.

Can you offer any advice or tips on breaking into television writing?
Nowadays your best chance is with a partner, so a show runner can get two writers for the price of one.

Diane Burroughs
Workshop Alum—Class of 1990
Executive Producer, *Still Standing*

Why did you choose to become a TV writer?
I chose to become a TV writer mostly because once I started reading various pilots and sample scripts, I thought, "I can do that." I'd always been a writer of one type or another and had done a lot of freelance journalism while living in Chicago. I had always pictured myself living and making a living in California, so it felt very natural to make the trek out here and give it a shot.

What was your first sample script, and how did you get someone to read it?
My partner, Joey Gutierrez, and I had written a *Cheers* that found its way to a friend of ours who knew someone in LA who was working on *Married with Children*. Her name was Ellen Fogle. She read our script and said we could come out and pitch ideas to *Married*. So, with no agent and a lot of butterflies in my stomach, I flew out to Los Angeles, just to pitch to her! Amazingly, she said she would "probably" give us a freelance episode that season. And based on her promise, Joey and I packed up a carload of our belongings and drove out to Los Angeles, with no place to stay and no real promise of employment! We then waited for the phone to ring for seven months, during which time I worked as an office temp and Joey went out on the road doing stand-up. Then the phone rang and it was *Married*, and they came through and gave us a freelance episode.

What do you look for in a sample script today?
What I look for in a script is: A joke on page 1. And every page after. You'd be amazed how many scripts have no jokes in the first five pages. And you know, with all the scripts we read, if it's not happening in those

first five pages, we move on to the next one. 'Cause believe me, there's always a next one.

What are the most common errors you have found in sample scripts?

The most common error in sample scripts is trying to change the core elements of the show they are trying to emulate. Many times young writers think they will impress someone if they introduce elements that are not normally done on that particular show, such as a new character or animation in a nonanimated show, etc. The best sample scripts really are just that—an episode that represents the world of that show in a fresh, funny way without compromising the intent and spirit of that particular show.

Can you offer any tips or advice for anyone trying to break into television writing?

I would say the hardest thing for writers breaking in is to believe in themselves, and to work hard, and to be relentless. Joey and I wrote fourteen sample scripts before we got our first staff job. Why so many? First of all, we were learning the form; second of all, agents need new scripts to submit each season and each midseason for staffing. So don't think you can write one script and send it out and get hired. Also, follow up with the people you do get meetings with. Drop them a note or stop by their set and watch an episode so you stay in their mind when it comes time to hand out that freelance assignment. Sometimes putting yourself out there is the hardest thing for those of us with a writer's personality. But you've got to learn to be comfortable with doing that, as this entire business is built on relationships.

Bruce Rasmussen
Executive Producer, *The Drew Carey Show*

Why did you choose to become a TV writer?
I started out thinking I would be a novelist. I began college as an English lit major, but I realized that at twenty-two I didn't really have the breadth or depth of experience to write novels. Film seemed more in keeping with what I thought I had to say, and so I went to film school at UCLA. I got an internship at MTM and met a bunch of writers on the *Newhart* show who took me under their wing. What really got me started was reading a pilot that had sold from some established writers that I thought was horrific. I thought, "I can definitely write better than that."

What was your first sample script, and how did you get someone to read it?
The first sample script I wrote was a *Newhart*. Since I was on the show as a production assistant and the writers liked me, they read it.

What do you look for in a sample script?
I look for something fresh. Since story is the hardest thing to learn, I look for jokes that don't look like jokes. Something with a more personal, specific tone. Personally I like more character-driven lines. Something that springs from a character's point of view, as opposed to a joke that anybody could say. On established shows it's easy to get a sense of who the characters are and how they think.

What are the common errors you have found in sample material?
Writing the same tired rhythms that bad television uses. Predictable jokes. Not starting from what a real person would say in that situation and trying to make that funny, trying to bend jokes to fit a situation or story.

Can you offer any tips or advice for anyone trying to break into television writing?

What I did and I suggest doing is watching a lot of television, good and bad, forming your own opinions about what's good and why and what's bad and why. Good writers are opinionated. I would also get my hands on actual scripts of television shows (they're available around town and on the Internet) and break them down into their basic structure, scene by scene, so you can see how a show is built. Television feels seamless or arbitrary sometimes watching it, but there are always reasons a well-written script makes the choices it does.

Mike Schiff

Executive Producer, *Grounded for Life* and *Third Rock From the Sun*

Why did you choose to become a TV writer?

Writing was something I aspired to (my father was an advertising copy-writer), and for whatever reason, I leaned to scriptwriting (rather than novels, essays, or journalism). While movies were part of this aspiration, I gravitated toward television because the idea of doing a new episode every week appealed to me. (Also, nobody wanted me to write their movies.) I prefer smaller, more personal stories, especially in comedy, and feature comedies tend (a broad generalization here) to be big, goofy constructs with outrageous high-concept premises. I preferred more human-sized stories. I met my writing partner, Bill Martin, in film school, where television was considered a lower form, but we secretly started writing sitcom scripts together.

What was your first sample script, and how did you get someone to read it?

Our first script was a *Cheers*, and we were able to get *nobody* to read it. We were living in New York at the time, which was an easy excuse for any LA agent to ignore us (they're so swamped, they'll take any excuse you provide them). We wrote a *Murphy Brown*, a *Dear John...*, a *Wings*, a *Seinfeld*... (the latter two after we'd moved to LA), but we still couldn't break in. (On the plus side, the scripts were getting better. We'd imagined our *Cheers* to be brilliant, but truth be told, practice was a plus.) Only when a well-liked exec at a small production company (whom we'd met socially) pitched us to a few agents did anybody bite. The agent we picked (she's still our agent today) was able to get us in the door at a sketch show, where we worked for two seasons. That led to two more sketch-show gigs, and soon we were typecast as sketch writers. But we wanted to do half hours! So we wrote yet another script (this one a *Frasier*). Eventually, we were able to break into the sitcom world.

What do you look for in a sample script today?
Above all, a coherent story with some element that surprises and an actual resolution that's earned. Obviously, it should also be funny, but a good (ideally, funny in its own right) premise that goes somewhere is the single most valuable commodity in the world of sitcoms. When you're trying to find a writing staff, agents bombard you with scripts. They become ubiquitous, like sand when you've been to the beach — you find them in your car, under your desk, in your bed, around your house . . . they seem to multiply. Eventually, they blur in your brain, and you begin to lose the sense of where one script ends and another begins. The only way to wake me up is with a story that has something to say (not something profound, necessarily, but at least a coherent sense of *why* this is a story worth telling), with a premise with a surprise or two that resolves satisfactorily. It's the hardest thing to find, but when you find it, you know it. (One particular script like this stood out to me in a pile I was reading while on the treadmill at the gym — not an ideal way to read a script, but its quality was obvious even in these conditions — and I wound up hiring the authors of this script at two different shows.)

What are the most common errors you have found in sample material?

Most of these are so easy to avoid, yet would-be writers consistently fail to avoid them.

Typos. Sure, we're not writing prose for publication here, but we are writers, and if you can't be bothered to proofread (or even run a spellchecker, for God's sake!), it shows a contempt for what it is we do. Writers who won't spend that minimal extra time announce themselves as lazy, which is not a good quality for a career where writers are expected to work until all hours until the script is right.

Length. A typical sitcom script, formatted correctly, is forty-six to fifty-two pages, fifty-five if you're generous. And yet I consistently receive scripts that are sixty-five pages or more. Writers too often contend, "I couldn't cut anything!" Well, yes you could. If you plan to write for network television, you must. The networks won't cut back on commercials because a writer couldn't cut any of his precious words. That's just how it is, and anyone who wants to be a writer should be expected to understand that. And a writer who finds his words that precious is likely to be a pain in the reality of week-in/week-out production.

Know the characters' names. This seems so incredibly obvious, yet writers rename regular characters in their scripts with some frequency.

Write about the characters. Too often, younger writers will bring in a colorful guest character (an old friend, a crazy cousin, a Mafioso) and relegate the series' regulars to background players reacting to this new creation. Television shows are about the main characters, not guest stars.

Don't be a smart-ass. It may seem outrageous to behead the main character or create a lesbian relationship between the two lead women. It's not. It's tedious. It's obvious. It's been done before. It's really just a lazy way out of doing the hard work of creating an actual usable story. And it fails to demonstrate even a tiny bit how you would write for a show where the main character cannot be beheaded. (By that same token, some writer had the bright idea a few years ago to write a script for a long-canceled series—a *That Girl* or the like. Well, I'll give that writer credit for a clever way to get noticed. But it has since become a genre unto itself; some agents call these "retrospecs," and they frequently feature similarly monotonous "outrageousness" involving sexual story lines that would have been forbidden at the time of the actual series. Yawn.)

One more thing: Struggling writers sometimes get it in their heads that insulting writer-producers is the way to get ahead. They'll send scripts with cover letters explaining that their fresh script is the key to revitalizing a show that has become tired, or contrived, or just plain bad. (This happens surprisingly often.) These people should realize that writer-producers generally do not like being called tired, contrived, or just plain bad—which makes this particular approach a very bad strategy.

Can you offer any tips or advice for anyone trying to break into television writing?
Realize that it's going to take time to break in. That your first sample probably isn't as good as you imagine; write another now. That it's not good enough for your script to be as good as some lousy show you just saw; it has to be better. And most important, that it has to be what you really want to do, because it's going to be plenty frustrating.

Bill Martin
Executive Producer, *Grounded for Life* and *Third Rock From the Sun*

Why did you choose to become a TV writer?
I am a goofy man with no organizational abilities, and I stopped developing emotionally at the age of fourteen. But I've always loved comedy, and some of the most defining moments of my youth were seeing Woody Allen movies and the Marx brothers and *Monty Python* and *Bob & Ray* and the *Mary Tyler Moore Show*, and it's all I've really ever wanted to do. I think if you consciously choose to become a comedy

writer, you face an uphill battle making it happen. With most of the good comedy writers I know, it was a calling that gripped them when they were young.

What was your first sample script, and how did you get someone to read it?

As Mike Schiff probably told you, it was a *Cheers*, and I don't think we ever actually got anybody to read it. A friend of mine went to high school with a woman at NBC, and I think the envelope with our script in it may have gotten as far as the wastebasket outside her office.

What do you look for in a sample script today?

Clear character voices and a story that unfolds in an interesting or surprising way. Pick a show that makes that possible. There are a lot of shows out there with characters that aren't clearly differentiated; you might write a dead-on sample, but if the characters all sound alike on the show, it'll be even more tedious on the page. That's why I like to read *Everybody Loves Raymond*, because a good writer can make a real impression with those distinctive character voices. Conventional wisdom says, "Don't write a pilot," but I like reading them; if they're good, they really show off a whole array of story and character skills.

What are the most common errors you have found in sample material?

It's amazing how many people don't proofread their scripts, and I find that galling. It tells readers that you feel you don't need to try hard, and unless you're the second coming of Larry David, that'll get your script a one-way ticket to the recycling bin. Lazy stories are also galling. So many writers will set up a premise, milk it for jokes, and then, when it runs out of gas, they'll just take a left turn and head off in another direction. Jokes are important, but jokes are irritating when they're strung along in lieu of an interesting story. Also, beware of using outside characters in a sample script. It's a crutch, and it suggests you don't know how to use the psychology of the show's main characters to generate a story.

Can you offer any tips or advice for anyone trying to break into television writing?

Do not send out a script until you have rewritten it at least eight times. (Or, like me, get an irritating, neurotic perfectionist for a partner.) If it's not the absolute best script you're capable of, you're only screwing yourself. People might say that they'll read your second script, or your fifth, but if the first one was lazy or slapdash, it's not going to happen. Be persistent, and don't hesitate to take a terrible job if it will get you closer to people who can read your stuff. And do not solicit notes from someone unless you intend to do a rewrite based on the notes, because you'll be sending that person the clear signal that you're just using them to get to an agent or show runner and you don't really care.

Jim Leonard

Executive Producer, *Skin* and *Thieves*

Why did you choose to become a TV writer?

Here's what I tell people: "The best writing in the world is on TV. The wittiest, the most moving, the most astonishing character work is all on TV. Why would I work anywhere else?" Here's the truth: I chose to work in TV because the writer has power in TV that he or she doesn't have in the movies. In TV, the writer hires and fires the director—not so in the movies. I chose to work in TV because it pays, and I have two children. Finally, and most important, I chose to work in TV because TV chose me. A writer-producer named Dan Pyne saw one of my plays and offered me a job.

What was your first sample script, and how did you get someone to read it?

My first script was a film adaptation of one of my plays. Robert Altman saw *The Diviners* on stage in New York and wanted to direct it as a film. He commissioned the script and taught me to write for the medium. I was lucky. My first TV script was a pilot for FOX that Ken Olin produced. It didn't go to series, but I learned a lot. I knew Ken Olin because his wife, Patricia Wettig, had been in two of my plays.

What do you look for in a sample script today?

I look for good writing. Period. I don't like scripts based on existing shows—I like original material. I want a writer to have a strong, distinctive voice. I want someone to tell me a good story. I read blind. No cover page. No idea if I'm reading a staff writer, a first-time writer, or someone with twenty years' experience in the business. I usually read the first five or ten pages, then skip to the middle and read some more. Once in a blue moon I get caught up and read the whole thing—that person usually gets hired.

What are the most common errors you have found in sample scripts?

Derivative writing. No one to care about. Overly cute, overly worked material. I hate writing where every line is a "line"—where it all feels written instead of stemming from passion.

Can you offer any tips or advice for anyone trying to break into television writing?

Write plays. Tell the truth.

Josh Schwartz
Executive Producer, *The O.C.*

Why did you decide you wanted to be a TV writer?

I have always loved TV and films equally and knew that TV was a much more inclusive medium for writers than features. As a writer in TV you get to be involved in everything—from casting to editing to the music—whereas in film you're usually much more of a hired gun.

What was your first sample script, and how did you get someone to read it?

My first feature script was called "Providence," which I wrote as a junior in college at USC Film School. I had a friend interning at a production company, and he showed it to his bosses, who showed it to a manager, who signed me and then sold the movie to Sony, where it has languished in development hell ever since. . . .

What do you look for in a sample script today?

I don't really read a lot of scripts . . . but you look for some sense of sparkle . . . that there is a point of view the writer has on the world . . . and that the voices of the characters have some snap, some intelligence to them. I also like to see if the writer has a sense of humor . . . but mostly that they take a show that's not theirs, and characters they didn't create, and make them their own. . . .

What are the most common errors you find in sample material?

The most common errors are the writers trying too hard to emulate what they think the show is and missing the point. I read a lot of *Six Feet Under* sample scripts where people think the key to that show is being outrageous or bizarre, and really I think people connect with that show for its honesty in portraying family dynamics and personal insecurities.

Same with *The Sopranos*; it's not all about the violence and swearing
. . . it's about the characters connecting with one another.

**Can you offer any tips or advice for anyone trying to break into
television writing?**

I would say as important as it is to have a great script, it's also important
to have an original piece of writing that really shows what you can do,
what your point of view on the world is. . . .

Leonard Dick
Workshop Alum—Class of 1995
Producer, *Tarzan*

Why did you decide you wanted to be a TV writer?

TV writing was a perfect fusion of two priorities for me: to live a creative
life and work in a collaborative setting (as opposed to screenwriting,
which is a more solitary endeavor). I wanted that fantasy experience of
the writers' room from the old *Dick Van Dyke Show*.

**What was your first sample script, and how did you get someone to
read it?**

My first sample script was a *Wonder Years* I wrote in a UCLA Extension
School sitcom-writing class. After I'd completed it, I matter-of-factly
mentioned what I was doing to a guy I'd recently become friendly with
socially, and he asked me to send it to him. He was something called a
"literary agent," which I knew nothing about. He read it, then called me
a week later to tell me I had a meeting at ABC.

What do you look for in a sample script today?

For sitcoms and family drama scripts, I love small stories that reveal
something new about the characters. I want to finish an *Everybody
Loves Raymond* and have learned something new and interesting about
Raymond and his relationship with Debra/Marie/Frank, etc.

For procedural-drama samples, I look for a neat area and a compelling human story that reflects back on our main characters. Plot twists and believable police work are certainly important, but I want to know why Mr. Smith murdered Ms. Jones—and more important, how the principal characters react to this. Why is Grissom so baffled by Mr. Smith's behavior when Willows is not? Why is Sarah so determined to nail Mr. Smith to the point that she's frustrated when the evidence reveals that maybe Mr. Smith isn't the killer? I also like a final-final twist as the last beat of the investigation. Mr. Smith killed Ms. Jones . . . but didn't know that Ms. Jones was planning to leave her husband to marry him.

What are the most common errors you find in sample material?
Forgetting the main characters—many writers introduce a guest character who becomes the focus of the episode. As the adage goes, the show is called *Everybody Loves Raymond,* not *Everybody Loves Raymond's New Colleague whom Raymond Is Trying to Fix Up.*

Stories too big and plots too complicated—simple stories, complex characters should be the rule. Stories should be easy to follow and allow the characters and relationships to breathe. In sitcoms particularly, reactions are often more interesting than actions.

Not going deep enough—a story should be more than just a plot; it should be rooted in an emotional truth or say something about human relations. It might be funny to see Frasier and Niles go to a rave, but why are they so determined to do this? Why is this so important to them?

Can you offer any tips or advice for anyone trying to break into television writing?
Give your script to anybody willing to read it—friends, neighbors, the guy at the deli counter, the mechanic at the car dealer . . . You never know who knows whom.

Keep writing—odds are your second script will be better than your first, your third better than your second, etc. This is the law of perpetual motion.

Write scripts for shows you like—the writing experience will be more enjoyable and the final product likely more compelling. Just because you hear everyone is writing a sample for *Show* X doesn't mean you should, particularly if you don't like *Show* X.

Most important of all: Think long term! That first break might not come right away, so don't get discouraged. Twenty years from now when you're sitting in your fancy executive producer office on the Warner Bros. lot, it won't make a difference whether it took you one, two, three, or more years to break in.

Jan Nash
Co-Executive Producer, *Without a Trace*

Why did you choose to become a TV writer?
I'm from a small suburb of Chicago and knew I wanted to be in the "entertainment" business. It took me a long time and a lot of other jobs to figure out what that meant. I loved writing. I was a compulsive journal writer and inflicted long, descriptive letters about my adventures on my friends, but it wasn't until I went to work at Disney's network TV department that I realized that people made a living writing for television.

What was your first sample script, and how did you get someone to read it?
My first script was a *Seinfeld,* and it was so horrible, I didn't let anyone read it. My second was a *Frasier,* also bad. It wasn't until my third script, a *Mad About You,* that I let anyone look at my stuff. I asked one of my colleagues, a man I knew was a kind reader, to take a look. He gave me a lot of notes and encouraged me to keep writing. (My first drama sample was a *Now & Again,* which got cancelled before I could ever send it out.)

What do you look for in a sample script today?
Passion. And a commitment to trying to get the show—whatever it is—right. A little bit of research about what works on a show and how they do what they do, plus a lot of rewriting, makes a huge difference. It's hard to write a script that "wows" people from front to back. Shooting for solid and readable, with a few splashes of personal flair, is a more doable goal and ultimately will yield a more successful script.

What are the most common errors you have found in sample material?
Bad format—it's amazing how the wrong font sticks in a reader's mind. Violations of show "rules" (such as not having the missing person in a *Without a Trace* flashback). Trying too hard to make it special and not concentrating enough on making it a good version of the show or just a good script.

Can you offer any tips or advice for anyone trying to break into television writing?
Write about things you care about. Write a lot. Don't get discouraged; the process of breaking in can be a slow one. Try to get into programs (like the one at Warner Bros.) that foster relationships with people in the industry. And try to remember—even though it's really, really hard to—that if you write, you're already a writer. Validation from others is nice, but not necessary.

Rina Mimoun
Executive Producer, *Everwood*

Why did you choose to become a TV writer?
I've loved watching TV since I was old enough to worship Desi Arnaz. And I loved playwriting in college. It seemed appropriate somehow to marry the two loves—writing and television.

What was your first sample script, and how did you get someone to read it?

My first sample script was a *Mad About You* called "Blonde Ambition" where Paul Reiser accidentally dyes his hair blonde. I was interning at a production company at the time, reading about twenty feature scripts a week for free. So when I got around to finishing my own script, my boss couldn't help but do me the favor, and then he helped me pass it on. Note to all employers: Free labor is never free.

What do you look for in a sample script today?

Humor. Pacing. An interesting story and whether or not the voices sound right. Structure is important, but you can learn that. Hearing the voices in your head and capturing them on the page—that's the hard part.

What are the most common errors you have found in sample material?

Spending too much time on very long runners that aren't funny enough to warrant the two-page setup.

Can you offer any tips or advice for anyone trying to break into television writing?

Love the show you sample. Don't write something just because some-one (even your agent!) tells you that's the one to do. Pick your favorite show where you can hear the people talking in your head, and go for it.

List of Television Terms
Bibliography
Resources

List of Television Terms

A-story: also known as the main story. Whether you are writing comedy or drama, the A-story focuses on the main character(s) of the show.

Act: a part of the format of a script or play. Comedies are broken into two acts or three acts; dramas are four. An act is broken down into scenes. Scenes are broken down into beats, or events. There are typically three or four beats per scene.

Act Break: the place in the script where the action reaches its highest point.

B-story or C-story: a subplot. A B-story may be a spinoff of the A-story and would involve secondary characters. A C-story would be a third story line and would not be given more time than either the A- or B-story.

Beat: an event; a moment when something happens. It can also be used as a dramatic pause. Example: "As he looked down at his feet for a beat, he explained why he was late."

Beat Sheet: a sheet of paper that contains all the beats of each story. It's the script's layout that is written prior to an outline.

Bible: a written presentation that describes the pilot episode, the characters, the overall premise, and the ideas for and the direction of future episodes.

Block Comedy Scene: the big physical comedic scene of a show, usually in act 2, before the resolution.

Blow: a funny joke that punctuates the end of a scene so it goes out on a laugh.

Brads: a small brass device used to bond scripts. Use two brads, one in each of the first and third holes of your script.

Broadcast Networks: better known as ABC, CBS, NBC, FOX, The WB, and UPN.

Button: see **Blow.**

Clam: a phrase that is overused and usually trendy that you should avoid using in dialogue. Examples include: "Houston, we have a problem," "Where's the beef?" "Talk to the hand," "Whazzzz upppp?"

Climax: the place in the script where the conflict has reached its most critical point. This is when the reader wonders how the character(s) is going to get out of this predicament.

Cold Open: the very first part of a show (even before the credits roll). For some shows it sets up part of what the story will be about, and sometimes it's unrelated (and funny if it's a sitcom). A cold open is also called a "teaser."

Conflict: the problem at hand. Every story has to have a conflict (something needs to actually happen).

Current Executive: an executive who works for a studio or network and is in charge of maintaining all episodes of the shows that they have been assigned.

Dailies: daily tapes from a drama or single-camera comedy show that is filmed on location prior to being edited. Executives review them in order to give notes, as they cannot be available to be on location at all times.

Development Executive: an executive who works for a production company, studio, or network and is responsible for developing ideas, casting, and production of new shows.

Development Season: the time of the year when credited individuals try to sell their show ideas to production companies, studios, and networks. For the major broadcast networks, development season starts in June and continues until January for drama and February for comedy series ideas. Many cable networks have eliminated development season because they are able to be more competitive by developing new shows all year-round.

Episodic Guide: a list of stories for a particular show already completed, available on a network's Web site.

Executive Producer(s): usually the creator and writer of a show. Other executive producers may include a star's manager or former studio or network executives turned producers. All executive producers have creative input and deal with the network directly, as they are the individuals responsible for the show on a daily basis.

Exposition: a written description of a character's feelings or attitudes that are not explained through dialogue.

EXT: specific formatting in body of script, meaning "exterior."

First Draft: the first fully written episode that has yet to be rewritten or polished.

Format: the way in which a script is written, with specified margins and other requirements that are standard in the industry.

INT: specific formatting in body of script, meaning "interior."

L.E.C.: "living end credit." An actual scene is playing while the credits are being shown.

Logline: one or two sentences that sum up the entire episode, with a clearly established beginning, middle, and end.

Main Titles: the graphics displayed on the screen of the names of the cast and the name of the show.

Multicamera Show: the use of four cameras on a soundstage to film a sitcom that is produced in front of a live studio audience.

Narrative: the details of a story line.

Notes: the process by which you listen to what people have to say about your script, then decide if listening to them is in the best interest of the material.

Original Material: either a play, feature film script, short story, treatment, or pilot script that was developed and written by you. Oftentimes, producers want to read a sample script and something that is original.

Outline: a detailed treatment of the stories you've chosen to write. Includes key dialogue and jokes (if writing a sitcom). You should always write an outline before writing a script.

Pilot: a first episode of a show. Pilots are used to determine if a network wants to order the show to series.

Pilot Script: the first episode script of a show. Sometimes pilot scripts are written before they are sold to a studio or network, but oftentimes a pitch is sold first and then the writer is paid to write the pilot script during the development season.

Pilot Season: the time of the year when pilots are ordered and filmed. For most networks, pilot season is January through May. In May, each network announces its new fall lineup.

Pitch: a writer's oral description of a show that he wants to sell to a studio or network or a story line he'd like to write for a show. Writers also pitch jokes to the show runner(s) to be included in the show.

Plot: the main action of a story.

Point of View (POV): a story told from one person's perspective.

Producer: the person who works on a show, either in a production capacity or as a writer.

PA: production assistant.

Resolution: the part of the script found in the last few scenes or the very final scene when everything gets worked out.

Runner: an incomplete story but functions like a completed one. It's usually found in comedy shows that use two story lines to add an additional layer and keeps coming up throughout the show.

Scene: the basic subunit of an act. An act is broken down into scenes, and the scenes can be various lengths.

Setup: the early part of a joke that is used to set up the upcoming funny part of the joke. Generally, one character will deliver the setup and another character delivers the punch line.

Show Runner: the person in charge of the writers who makes all the final decisions with regards to the show. Also see **Executive Producer.**

Single-camera Comedy: shows like *Sex and the City, Scrubs,* and *Malcolm in the Middle* that are filmed on location, rather than in front of a studio audience on a soundstage. There is no audience laughter on a single-camera show.

Slug Line: a line in the script that determines the place and time of each scene and perhaps a description of the action.

Staffing Season: the period of time when agents send out their writer clients' material to executive producers and studio and network executives to be considered for writing jobs on shows.

Story Subtext: the part of a script revealing a character's thoughts and feelings.

Structure: the format in television that is specifically designed to tell your story. A sitcom is usually structured in two acts, whereas a drama is structured in four acts.

Syndication: shows eligible for rerun status after airing for four years when they have achieved approximately eighty-eight episodes. A fee is paid to the producing studio to air these shows in various cities around the country in addition to any original episodes (if the show is still in production). There are other shows that are originally sold into syndication. Those that are scripted are dramas, whereas those that aren't scripted are talk shows and game shows.

Table Read: the actors of a show read a new script for the first time so that everyone involved in the show can "hear" the dialogue being spoken. After notes are given on the script, the writers rewrite pages or the entire script.

Tag: a scene or situation found at the end of the script. It may tie up loose ends of a story line or a runner and is usually just a page long. A funny, poignant tag can create a good chuckle, resulting in the reader finishing on a high note.

Teaser: shown just before the show's theme song is played and the show's title page (show's name) appears on-screen. It may begin on an upcoming story line or have no relation to the story. It should read funny (if for a comedy), wanting the reader to read on or the viewer to keep watching.

Treatment: the narrative written version of the characters and stories for your proposed script.

Tree Analogy: a commonly used device to show the progression of an episode, from initial obstacle in the first scene to resolution in the last.

Twist: a turn in the story that happens unexpectedly. Twists are needed to add suspense and jeopardy in a drama and conflict and irony in a comedy script. Plot twists and turns are what hook an audience and keep them tuning in week to week.

Voice-over: the narration by a performer of information, feelings, or events as if he or she is observing while footage is being shown. Also used in cartoons as the voice of the character. For example, J.D. in *Scrubs* uses voice-over to tell the audience what he's thinking or what is going on.

Widow: the block of copy that may be cut if it is determined that it repeats a story point from an earlier (or later) scene.

Bibliography

Blum, Richard A. *Television Writing from Concept to Contract.* Revised ed. Stoneham, Mass.: Focal Press, 1984.

Brooks, Tim, and Earle Marsh. *The Complete Directory to Primetime Network and Cable TV Shows, 1946-Present.* 7th ed. New York: Ballantine, 1999.

DiMaggio, Madeline. *How to Write for Television.* New York: Prentice Hall, 1990.

Lucey, Paul. *Story Sense: Writing Story and Script for Feature Film and Television.* New York: McGraw-Hill, 1996.

Mascello, Robert. *A Friend in the Business: Honest Advice for Anyone Trying to Break into Television Writing.* 1st ed. New York: Perigee Books, 2000.

Wolff, Jurgen. *Successful Sitcom Writing: How to Write and Sell for TV's Hottest Format.* 2d ed. New York: St. Martin's Press. 1996.

Resources

Places to rent tapes in person or by mail

Eddie Brandt's Saturday Matinee
Has almost every movie and TV series on tape.
5006 Vineland Avenue
North Hollywood, CA
818-506-4242

PBS VideoFinders
Costs two dollars for the first minute and one dollar each additional. They can
tell you where to find a video, how much it costs, and so on. Average call lasts
three minutes.
900-860-9301

Places to watch tapes

Academy of Television Arts and Sciences (ATAS)
5220 Lankershim Blvd.
North Hollywood, CA 91601-3109
818-754-2800
www.emmys.org

Museum of Radio & Television
Has more than one hundred thousand radio and TV programs to review.

Museum of Radio & Television in New York
25 West Fifty-second Street
New York, NY 10019
212-621-6600

Museum of Radio & Television in Los Angeles
465 North Beverly Drive
Beverly Hills, CA 90210
310-786-1000
www.mtr.org

Writers Guild of America, East
555 West Fifty-seventh Street, Suite 1230
New York, NY 10019
212-767-7800
www.wgaeast.com

Writers Guild of America, West
7000 West Third Street
Los Angeles, CA 90048
323-951-4000
800-548-4532
www.wga.org